TABLE OF CONTENTS
SCRIPTURE TEXT 4

SCRIPTURAL TEXT

"For I have not shunned to declare unto you all the counsel of God." Acts 20:27

Introduction to 1st Timothy

1st and 2nd Timothy and Titus are commonly referred to as "The Pastoral Epistles." These are letters to Timothy (at Ephesus) and Titus (at Crete) concerning the pastoral care of the churches.

Paul wrote Timothy to exhort himself to defend the purity of the Gospel and its holy standard and to protect it from false teachers. He also wrote concerning his ministry and personal life.

Paul communicates to his younger assistant to earnestly contend for the faith and refute the false teachings that were diluting the True Gospel message of salvation in Jesus Christ.

Paul also instructs Timothy on how to relate to various groups such as: Women (2:9-15; 5:2), Widows (5: 3-16), Older and younger men (5:1), Women (2:9-15; 5:2), Widows (5: 3-16), Older and younger men (5:1), 19).

Finally, Paul conveys affection for Timothy as his convert and son in the faith and sets forth a high standard of godliness for his life and for the church.

"Paul, an apostle of Je'sus Christ by the commandment of God our Saviour, and Lord Je'sus Christ which is our hope;"
"Unto Tim'o-thy, my own son in the faith: Grace, mercy, and peace, from

God our Father and Je'sus Christ our Lord."
1: 1-2

Paul's credentials w ere unquestionable. He was commissioned from God our Savior even, our Lord Jesus. We must understand the use of [Kai]. The word translated "and" is from the Greek word Kai. It can be translated as "and' or as "even". The salutations do not indicate any distinction of persons in God. At the most, the use of Kai in these cases denotes a distinction of roles, manifestation, or names by which humans know God. Kai actually identifies Jesus as the same being as God, the same being as the Father.

God is our Lord (Isaiah 43:11; 45:21; 60:16). And of course we know Jesus is our Savior (Titus 2:13; 3:6). We only have one Savior; therefore, they are one in the same. Our hope is in Jesus… *"Christ in you, the hope of Glory,"* Our hope of eternal life is built upon Jesus.

Paul called Timothy his son because he served with him in the gospel. He sends grace, mercy and peace to Timothy from God our Father and [Kai] even Jesus Christ our Lord. Ministers in the gospel need more of God's mercy, while they dispense the gospel.

"As I besought thee to abide still at Eph'e -sus, when I went into Mac-edo'ni-a, that thou mightiest charge some that they teach no other doctrine,"

"Neither give heed to fables and endless genealogies, which minister questions, rather than godly edifying which is in faith: so do."
1: 3-4

Although Timothy wanted to go with Paul to Macedonia, Paul asked him to stay at Ephesus. False teachers were distorting the true Gospel message in Jesus (Acts 20:29). The wolves did enter in to undermine the apostolic doctrine at Ephesus.

Paul exhorted Timothy not to compromise with these false teachers. He must wage a good warfare against them (v.8).

Ministers must not only promote the True Gospel message in Jesus, but, they must also charge others not to preach any other doctrine except what Paul and the other apostles had taught (Gal. 1:8-9).

Neither give heed (prosecho 4337) "attended unto" *fables and endless genealogies."* There were some teachers who were bringing Judaism into Christianity. Things that do not edify the church, pulls it down. All these other teachings other than the apostles' tend to shake the foundation of a

Christians hope in Jesus, Godly edifying must be in faith. The Gospel is the foundation we build on and Jesus is the chief corner stone.

"Now the end of the commandment is charity out of a pure heart, and of a good conscience, and of faith unfeigned:"
"From which some having swerved have turned aside unto vain jangling;"
1: 5-6

Instructions from God's Word are not only biblical knowledge, but an inward moral transformation. One which expresses love, a clear conscience and faith unfeigned (anupokritos 505) "without dissimulation" "without hypocrisy, a conscience void of offence.

A good conscience involves an inner freedom of spirit. When our conscience is defiled, our communion with God is in jeopardy, the result, a shipwreck of our faith.

By our love for one another all men will know we are of God, His disciples (Jn. 13:35). We must preach the Gospel message with love, love from a pure heart, a heart purified by faith, purified from corrupt affections.

Now some who set themselves up as teachers have turned away unto vain jangling. When a minister turns from the law oflove, they'll give heed to "vain jangling." (Vain talking that profits nothing).

Those who deal in vain communication are found zealous to be teachers of others; they desire the office of a teacher. Yet they are very ignorant about what they are teaching. They do not understand what they themselves say; nor whereof they affirm.

"Desiring to be teachers of law; understanding neither what they say, nor whereof they affirm."
"But we know that the law is good, if a man use it lawfully;"

"Knowing this, that t he law is not made for a righteous man, but for the lawless and disobedient, for the ungodly and for sinners, for unholy and profane, for murderers of fathers and murderers of mothers, for manslayers,"

"For whoremongers, for them that defile themselves wit h mankind, for menstealers, for liars, for perjured persons, and if there be any other thing that is contrary to sound doctrine;"
1: 7-10

The law is good if used properly. However, the Jews used it to divide the church. The abuse that some have used of the law does not take away the use of it. Though we are not under the law, we certainly can learn from it. The law was not made for a righteous man but for the wicked. It is the grace of God that changes a persons' heart not the law.

The law and covenant were not complete, nor were they intended to be permanent. The law was a temporary tutor for God's people until Jesus came (Gal 3: 22-26). The old covenant was replaced with a new one. In which God's plan of salvation in Jesus was revealed (Rom. 3: 24-26).

"According to the glorious gospel of the blessed God, which was committed to my trust."
1:11

Paul reckoned it a great honor to have been entrusted with the gospel, the preaching of it. The ministry is a trust, for the gospel was committed unto the apostles. Real ministers are called stewards, (1Cor. 4:1), because we are over the trust (ministry). To be found faithful unto the gospel of our Lord Jesus Christ, in this great trust, is an awesome responsibility.

"And I thank Christ Je'sus our Lord, who hath enabled me, for that he counted me faithful, putting me into the ministry;"
1:12

True ministers of God, who speak the Word of God in truth, under the anointing of God, do so to please Him, and not men. They are called by Him and not by men. Those who God calls, He also qualifies them for their position in His church.

We, who are called, appointed, and anointed in the church of God, ought to give thanks to our Lord Jesus Christ for finding us worthy of such a heavenly vocation. Especially when we look at what we were before, (i.e. a liar, murderer, thief, a sinner etc.) but we obtained mercy in Jesus name.

"Who was before a blasphemer, and a persecutor, and injurious: but I obtained mercy, because I did it ignorantly in unbelief."
1:13

Although Paul was a blasphemer, persecutor, and injurious to the church, he obtained mercy for what he did before his conversion on the church, he obtained mercy for what he did before his conversion on the 2, 4-5, 22:4-5, 26:9-11, Gal. 1:13).

"And in the grace of our Lord was exceeding abundant with faith and love

which is in Christ Je'sus."
1:14

Paul recognizes the abundance of grace he received from Jesus. God has given a measure of grace to everyone (unbelievers) in order for them to be saved (1Cor. 14; Eph. 2:8-9; Titus 2:11). God has manifested His grace, mercy and love through Jesus (Jn. 3:16; 1Cor. 15:10; Phil. 2:13).

"This is a faithful saying, and worthy of all acceptation, that Christ Je'sus came into the world to save sinners; of whom I am chief.
1:15

Here we have the integral of the Gospel in a nut shell. God, through His mercy and grace, for His love of mankind manifested Himself in the flesh, took upon our nature, was made flesh, and dwelt among us (Jn.1:14). *"He came to the world not to call the righteous but sinners to repentance"* (Matt. 9:13).

It is a faithful saying, which needs to be embraced by faith in Jesus, it is worthy of all acceptation, therefore received with all love.

Paul acknowledges that he was a top sinner, worst of the worse. He realizes where the grace of God has brought him from. Jesus came to save all sinners, all who would call upon Him in sincere repentance.

"Howbeit for this cause I obtained mercy, that in me first Je'sus Christ might shew forth all longsuffering, for a pattern to them which should hereafter believe onhim to life everlasting."

1:16

First note Paul was one of the first great sinners converted to Christianity. A blasphemer, murderer, a persecutor of the church of Jesus Christ, yet God showed him mercy, because he done the things through ignorance.

Second, he obtained this mercy not just for himself but others as well. He set an example. No matter how great your sins are Jesus will forgive you, if you call upon Him with a sincere heart in true repentance.

Thirdly, our Lord Jesus was long suffering when dealing with Paul, just as He is with us. Not willing that any should perish, but that all should come to repentance (2Pet. 3:9).

Fourth, those who obtain mercy believe on the Lord Jesus, *" Without faith it is impossible to please God,"* (Heb. 11:6). He will reward those who diligently seek Him. He is our shield and our exceeding great reward (Gen. 15:1; Jn. 14:21. Matt. &:7-8).

Fifth, those who believe on Jesus Christ place their faith in Him and have a hope of eternal life with Him (Heb. 10.39).
"Now unto the King eternal, immortal, invisible, the only wise God, be honour and glory for ever and ever. Amen."
1:17

Jesus is the "King Eternal." He is eternal, immortal and everlasting (Deut. 33:27; Is. 9:6). He is the First and the Last (Rev. 1:8). He had no beginning and will have no ending. Other spiritual beings, including humans, are immortal as far as the future is concerned but only God is eternal in the past and the future.

God is a Spirit He is invisible unless He chooses to reveal Himself in some form whereby we can see Him. No man has seen God at anytime (Ex. 33:20; 1Tim. 6:16). However, when we see Jesus, we see God in the face of Jesus. You will not see God outside of Jesus.

God has complete knowledge of everything, including foreknowledge of future events (Acts 2:23). Like omnipresence, omniscience, omnipotence these attributes belong to God. Yet the Word of God says all these belong to Jesus. He is the "Wise God." All honor and glory belong to Him. He has all power in heaven and in the earth (Matt. 28:18). Jesus is the Ancient of Days (Dan.7:9). He is the immortality (6:16) for He cannot die.

"This charge I commit unto thee, son Tim'o -thy, according to the prophecies which went before on thee, that thou by them mightiest war a good warfare;"

"Holding faith, and a good conscience; which some having put away concerning faith have made shipwreck:"
"Of whom is Hy-menae'us and Al-exan'der; whom I have delivered unto Sa'tan, that they may learn not to blaspheme."
1:18-19-20

Paul charged Timothy to remain faithful to the revealed will of God in his life. As a pastor he must remain loyal to the Apostolic Doctrines and wage a good warfare against the false teachers who had crept into the church.

" Holding faith and a good conscience." We must hold to the True Word of God, and keep our conscience clear of offences. Those who put away a good conscience will shipwreck their faith, like Hyneneus and Alexander.

Apparently these two were part of the true church of God and they had turned their back on it. Paul warns Timothy several times of the possibility of personal apostasy (4:1; 5:11-15; 6:9-10).

Paul said he delivered Hyneneus and Alexander to Satan, which means they were probably excommunicated from the church.
"I exhort therefore, that, first of all supplications, prayers, intercessions, and giving of thanks, be made for all men;"
2:1
Paul exhorts not only Timothy, but the church as well, to pray for all men in general, especially those in authority.
Supplications (deh-ay-sis1162) "Petition or request"
Prayers (proseuche 4335) "an asking, entreaty"
Intercessions (enteuxis 1783) "a lighting upon, meeting with" Seeking the presence and hearing of God on behalf of others.

Supplications for the averting of evil, prayers for the obtaining of good, intercessions for others, and thanksgiving for mercies received. *"Pray always with all prayer*: (Eph. 6:18). *"Pray without ceasing"* (1Thess. 5:17). Pray for all men even our enemies (Matt. 5:44).

"For kings, and for all that were in authority; that we may lead a quiet and peaceable life in all godliness and honesty." "For this is good and acceptable in the sight of God our Saviour;" 2: 2-3

Although in Paul's lifetime the kings were pagan and they despised Christians Paul exhorted Timothy to pray for them. This is just as true today for us. We need to pray not only for our leaders in our country but all leaders. Pray they make the right decisions, and for their welfare.

What do we pray for them? That they might lead a quiet and peaceable life, in all "godliness and honesty." Godliness, the right to worship God, honesty, a good conduct toward all men. If we are to live quiet and peaceful lives it must be done in all godliness and honesty.

The reason we pray like this is because *"it is good and acceptable in sight of God our Savior."* We gave only one Savior, this is Jesus Christ (Jn. 3:16-17).

"Who will have all men to be saved, and to come unto the knowledge of truth."
2:4
God promises salvation to all who call upon Him, who are willing to forsake

their sin (repentance) and obey His Word (Ez. 18:23). God wants everyone to come to the knowledge of the truth of the gospel. He doesn't desire anyone to perish (2Pet. 3:9; Ez.33:11; Jonah 3:10). God's perfect will is that He desires all to be saved. His permissive will, is He permits many to refuse salvation in Jesus if they so desire (Matt. 7:21; Luke 7:30; Jn. 7:17; Acts 7:51).

"For there is one God, and one mediator between G od and men, the man Christ Je'sus;"
2:5

Paul does make a distinction in God in this verse, but a distinction between God and the man Jesus Christ. It is not God who mediates between God and mankind. It is the man Jesus who mediates, only a sinless man could approach a holy God on behalf of mankind.

Only through Jesus can we obtain true fellowship with God.

The only way we could be reconciled with God and understand Him is through His manifestation in flesh, through the sinless man Jesus Christ. When we are one with Jesus, we are one with God. No one comes unto the Father (God) except by Jesus (Jn. 14:6; 2Jn. 9). *"To wit, that God* (the spirit) *was in Christ* (the flesh, the man) *reconciling the world* (us) *unto himself"* (2Cor. 5:19). Jesus was both God and man. He was/is our mediator and high priest (Heb. 2:16-18; 4:14-16).

"Who gave himself a ransom for all, to be testified in due time."
2:6

Ransom (antilitron 4870) "equivalence," "on behalf of." Jesus gave Himself on behalf of us (all mankind). Through the death of Jesus on the cross we have been released from condemnation (Rom. 3:25-26), sin (Eph. 1:7), and death (Rom. 8:2). This "Ransom" is appropriated to all who call upon Him in true repentance. The offering of Jesus' blood on the cross was:

1) Sacrifice (1Cor. 5:7; Eph. 5:2)
2) It was vicarious: He died for our sake not His (Rom. 5:8; 8:32)
3) It was substitution, He died in our place (Rom.6:23)
4)It was propitiatory, His death for us satisfied God's wrath against the sinner (2Cor. 5:19; Jn.3:16; 1Cor. 8:6)
5) It was expiatory, a sacrifice to atone or make reparation for sin, the power of sin annulled.
6) It was efficacious, was effective as a means for our salvation.

7) It was victorious, a triumph over sin, death and Satan.

By the "Ransom" of Jesus' own lif e He liberated us from the enemies of our soul, (sin-death-Satan). Jesus saved us from death and hell. Sin had separated us from God. Jesus as our mediator repaired the breach, and reconciled us back to God, through His blood.

"Whereunto I am ordained a pr eacher, and an apostle, (I speak the truth in Christ, and lie not;) a teacher of the Gen'tiles in faith and verity."
2:7

Paul was ordained by God to preach to the Gentiles the message of redemption and salvation in Jesus Christ. He was appointed an apostle to teach the Gentiles.

Paul an ordained minister by God himself sent to declare that Jesus is the one and only mediator between God and men, who gave Himself a "Ransom" for all Whether Jew or Gentile, bond or free, rich or poor. This message that all true men of God are supposed to proclaim until Jesus comes back for His church. Jesus is not only our mediator, our High Priest, our Savior, but the True Living God, the only wise God.

"I will therefore that men pray every where, lifting up holy hands without wrath and doubting."
2:8

Paul exhorts the church to keep a praying spirit. Pray everywhere, at home, work, school, anywhere and everywhere. Prayer is not just confined to our churches or a wall. Nor are we restricted to 5 times a day. We can pray always, anytime while lifting up holy hands, pure hands, free from sin and pray with love *"Without wrath,"* or malice or anger toward any person. Pray in faith without doubting (James 1:6). *"The effectual fervent prayer of a righteous man availeth much,"* (James 5:16).

Prayer must be made in the name of Jesus (Jn. 14:13-14). Our prayers must be according to the will of God (1Jn. 5:14; Matt. 6:10; Luke 11:2).

"In like manner also, that women adorn themselves in modest apparel, with shamefacedness ad sobriety; not with braided hair, or gold, or pearls, or costly array;"

"But (which becometh wromen professing godliness) with good works."
"Let the woman learn in silence with all subjection."
"But I suffer not a woman to teach, nor to usurp authority over man but to be

in silence."
2: 9-12

Women who profess to be a Christian should be modest, and sober, with shamefacedness.

Modest (Kosmios 2887("orderly, well-arranged, decent, modest." Shamefacedness (aidos 127) a sense of shame, modesty is used regarding the demeanor of women in the church.

Sobriety (sophrosune 4997) "soundness of mind," "sound judgment." It is that habitual inner self-government, with its constant rein on all the passions and desires.

It is God's will that women dress discreetly. Keep their bodies covered, as not to draw attention to themselves from the opposite sex. That it doesn't provoke immoral desires or lust in others (Gal. 5:13; Eph. 4:27; Titus 2:11-12; Matt. 5:28; 1Pet. 3:2-3).

The word shamefacedness implies a certain shame in exposing the body. The sourceof modesty is in a person's heart. Modesty is the outward manifestation of a Holy God who created purity on the inside.

Braided (plegna 4117) "plaiting," is used in braiding hair with ringlets, adornments, intertwining within the hair, with gold or other articles of luxury.

Women must learn the Word of God; their sex is not an excuse for learning the necessities of the Word, especially of salvation. They must be submissive, because:

"For Ad'am was first formed, then Eve."
"And Ad'am was not deceived, but the woman being deceived was in the transgression."
2: 13-14

Adam was formed first. God created man first, thus we can readily see God's placement of leadership in the family. The woman was created to be a help meet for man, a companion. And Eve being a weaker vessel partook of the forbidden fruit and gave to Adam. Adam neglecting his leadership position given to him by God, consented to Eve's sin and mankind fell. This fall brought death to the entire human race.

Adam was not deceived, not first anyway. But the woman (Eve) was first in transgression (2Cor. 11:3). As God is head of Jesus, Jesus head of man, and man head of woman. The word head expresses authority and origination. This subordination is not demeaning to the woman. The man must recognize the worth God places on women. The man's responsibility is to protect, provide and lead the woman in the ways of God. She is not a second class person.

"Notwithstanding she shall be saved in childbearing, if they continue in faith and charity and holiness with sobriety."
2:15

Women will be saved by faith in Jesus just like everyone, and by accepting her punishment as the transgression she committed in the Garden of Eden. There is no greater honor, joy or delight than that of a Christian wife and mother (5:14). The honor of child-bearing is not to be depreciated by a Christian. It was not meant to demean women who are not married or unable to bear children (1Cor. 7:34).

Women are to profess godliness as well as men; they are baptized in Jesus' name, and filled with God's Spirit, thereby stand engaged to exercise themselves to godliness.

"This is a true saying, If a man desire the office of a bishop, he desireth a good work."
"A bishop them must be blameless, the husband of one wife, vigilant, sober, of good behavior, given to hospitality, apt to teach;" 3:1-2

The office of a bishop is an office of divine appointment not of human intervention. This office was bestowed upon the church by Jesus (Eph. 4:8-11). The office of a bishop requires diligence and application in the Word of God. The ministry was appointed to open men's eyes, turn them from darkness to light and bring many sins into glory. In order to be appointed in the office, the workman must be blameless, the husband of one wife, vigilant, sober, of good behavior, given to hospitality, apt to teach, not given to wine, no striker, not greedy, not a brawler, nor covetous.

Blameless (anepileptos 423) "that cannot be laid hold of," hence, "not open to censure, irreproachable" "without reproach"
Vigilant (nephalios 3524) "temperate" "of sound mind," "self-control," "circumspect"
Sober (sophron 4998) "of sound mind" always rendered "sober-minded"
Good Behavior (Kosmios 2887) "orderly, modest" both have "modest" in (of good behavior)
Hospitality (philoxenos 5382) "hospitable" receiving or treating guest or strangers warmly and generously.

Apt to teach (didaktikos 1317) "skilled in teaching" or "to give instruction
Striker (plektes 4131) "To strike," smites, to fight a brawler.
Filthy lucre(aischrokerdes 146) denotes "greedy of base gains" a "to gain, get gain"
Brawler (amachos 269) "Not fighting" a "not contentious"
Covetous (aphilarguros 866) "free from the love of money," or "no lover of money"
Patient (epieikes) "Gentle" in contrast to contentiousness
"Not given to wine, no striker, not greedy of filthy lucre; but patient, not a brawler, not covetous;"
3:3

Not given to wine (GK Mi paroinon, from mi, meaning "not," and paroinos, a compound meaning "at, by, near, next to, or with wine). The Word states that no overseer or elder may *"sit beside wine"* or *"be with wine."* In other words, he should not partake of an intoxicating beverage. *"Nor eat and drink with the drunken"* (Matt. 24:49).

Those who rule in the church must have high standards. Furthermore, all believers in the church are called priests and kings (1Pet. 2:9; Rev. 1:6).

A minister must be vigilant, because our adversary the devil goes about like a roaring lion, seeking whom he may devour (1Pet. 5:8). He must be sober, temperate, always watching out for his flock, and given to hospitality, ready to lend a helping hand not only to his brothers in Christ but to strangers as well.

A minister must also be ready to teach the Word of God in all diligence and patience, to communicate to others that which God has entrusted him with, the full council of God. Not a contentious minister, rather one who possesses gentleness, love and mildness.

"One that ruleth well his own house, having his children in subjection with all gravity;"
"(For if a man know not how to rule his own house, how shall he take care of the church of God?)"
3: 4-5

A Bishop must be one who ruleth well in his own house. That he may set the example for other ministers to follow. If a man cannot take care of his own house, how then can he pastor a church?

The church of today must not turn from the righteous requirements for an overseer which God has set forth. The church must choose a leader who is a walking, talking, living man of God. One who sets the example of godly living, by his lifestyle.

"Not a novice, lest being lifted up with pride he fall into the condemnation of the devil."
"Moreover he must have a good report of them which are without; lest he fall into reproach and the snare of the devil."
3: 6-7

Not a novice (neophutos 3504) "Newly -planted" (from neos, "New," and phuo, "to bring forth, produce"). Denotes "a new convert, neophyte, novice," one who is inexperienced is unfit to act as an overseer or bishop in a church.

He must know more than surface religion, for such a one may be lifted up in pride. Pride was the fall of Satan. A bishop must be of good reputation among all men.

One who desires to become a Bishop must " *have a good report*" with both those in the church and those outside the church. He must live and conduct his life according to the Gospel of Jesus Christ.

"Likewise must the deacons be grave, not doubletongued, not given to much wine, not greedy of filthy lucre;"
3:8

The deacons (ck diakonos 1249) a "servant" The deacons are to assist the pastor/bishop by attending to the temporal and material affairs of the church. So the Bishop can devote more time to prayer and the ministry of the Word (Acts 6:4). The qualifications are the same as pastors (Acts 6:3; vv. 1-7, 8-13).

He must be grave. (semnos 4586) first denoted "reverend, august, and venerable." Gravity becomes all Christians, but especially those in office.

Not double- tongued; that will say one thing to one and another thing to another. Of course not given to wine, it is reprehensible to think that a leader in the church would be drunk with fermented alcoholic beverages. Drunkenness is a terrible sin that will exclude one from the Kingdom of God (1Cor. 6:10; Gal. 5:19; Eph. 5:5; Heb. 12:14).

"Holding the mystery of the faith in a pure conscience."
3:9

A pure conscience is achievable, if one commits themselves to God and forsakes the world. In doing this they will be, *"holding the mystery of faith in a pure conscience."* The mystery of the faith implies several things:

1) The mystery was proclaimed by Paul to the Gentiles. The Gospel message is available to one and all.
2) God manifested Himself in the flesh.
3) Christ in us is our hope of glory

Bear in mind once the mystery is revealed it is no longer a mystery. *"And let these also first be proved; then let them use the office of a deacon, being found blameless."*
"Even so must their wives be grave, not slanderers, sober, faithful in all things."
3: 10-11

No one should just step into these offices (Bishop- Deacon-Etc.) without first proving themselves. The soundness of their judgments, their zeal for Jesus, a blameless conversation, they must be proven in these areas.

Good behavior, not slanderers, tale-bearers, gossipers as to sow discord in the church. They must be sober and faithful in all areas of their lives. The husband of one wife and rule well in their own household, they too must be examples for others to follow.

"Let the deacons be the husbands of one wife, ruling their children and their own houses well."

"F or they that have used the office of a deacon well purchase to themselves a good degree, and great boldness in the faith which is in Christ Je'sus."
3:12-13

The office of a deacon may be a lower office; however, it is a step towards the higher office (Bishop) eventually. Although they may serve tables now, in the future they'll have opportunity to minister the Word of God.

There are two offices mentioned here in the church: Bishops and Deacons. The office of the Bishop was mainly confined to prayer and ministering the Word of God. The Deacons serving tables, assisting the Bishop, they as well as the Bishop must walk circumspectly.

"These things write I unto thee, hoping to come unto thee shortly:"

"But if I tarry long, that thou mayest know how thou ou ghtest to behave

thyself in the house of God, which is the church of the living God, the pillar and ground of the truth."

3:14-15

Paul's heart's desire was to see Timothy soon to give him more directions to assist him in his ministry work. The leaders of the house of God need to know how to conduct themselves as to not bring reproach upon the house of God. Ministers need to behave themselves well not just in prayer and ministering the Word, but in their behavior as becometh a Christian, a man of God.

As the church of God it is the pillar and ground truth. We must keep and preserve the truth, the Apostles Doctrine. *"Buy the truth and sell it not"* (Prov. 23:23). The church must be the foundation of the truth of the Gospel. The church upholds the truth revealed in Jesus and the apostles by receiving and obeying it (Matt. 13:23) hiding it in our hearts (Ps. 119:11) proclaiming the word of life (Phil. 2:16), defending it (Phil. 1:17) contending for it (Jude 3). Just what is the truth which the church and ministers are the pillars and grounds of?

"And without controversy great is the mystery of godliness: God was manifest in the flesh, justified in the Spir'it, seen of angels, preached unto the Gen'tiles, believed on in the world, received up into glory."

3:16

God was manifested (made visible) in the flesh; God was justified (shown to be right in the Spirit; God was seen of angels; God was believed on in the world; and God was received up into glory. When did all of this happen? In Jesus Christ.

" In the beginning was the Word, and the Word was with God, and the Word was God…. And the Word was made flesh, and dwelt among us" (Jn. 1:1; 14). Literally, the Word (God) was tabernacle in the flesh of Jesus among us. Both these verses prove Jesus is Godthat He is God manifested (revealed, made known, made evident, displayed, shown) in flesh.

Jesus is the Son of God – God in flesh (Matt. 1:21-23). He has a dual nature, human and divine, or flesh and Spirit.

The complete deity and humanity are united inseparably in the person Jesus.

He who was manifest in flesh was God, really and truly God, and God by nature; this makes it to be a mystery. However, this mystery has been revealed.

"Now the Spir'it speaketh expressly, that in the latter times some shall depart from the faith, giving heed to seducing spirits, and doctrines of devil;"

4:1

In the previous verse 3:16 we had the mystery of godliness revealed. Now Paul says some shall depart from the faith. Now we see a prophecy of the mystery of iniquity in the latter times. Some shall depart from the faith, the faith delivered to the saints (Jude 3), the sound doctrine, the apostles' doctrine.

John said the anti-Christ spirit went out from the church. These were at one time in the truth, the apostles' doctrine, but later departed from the truth (1Jn. 2:19). They abandoned their faith.

The Spirit has revealed that there would be a falling away from the faith, John seen this. They may have been mighty men in the church. However, they will turn from the faith unto seducing spirits and false doctrines. *"Many will fall away from the faith, because they will not love the truth"* (2Thess. 2:10).

"Speaking lies in hypocrisy; having their conscience seared with a hot iron;"

"Forbidding to marry, and commanding to abstain from meats, which God hath created to be received with thanksgiving of them which believe and know the truth."

"For every creature of God is good, and nothing to be refused, if it be received with thanksgiving:"

"For it is sanctified by the word of God and prayer."

4: 2-5

The propagating of these damnable doctrines of devils will be through lies of hypocrisy. A pretentiousness of godly miracles will lead many astray.

Seared (kausteriazo 2743) "to burn with a branding iron" The reference is to apostles whose consciences are "branded" with the effects of their sin.

Another characteristic of an apostate, false teacher is the forbidding of marriage and that they abstain from meats.

Men and women must have their hearts hardened and their consciences seared, before they can depart from the True Gospel. It is a noticeable sigh when some depart when they do what is forbidden by God.

What God has created is to be received with thanksgivin g. *"What God hath cleansed, that call not thou common"* (Acts 10:15). *"Every creature of God is good and nothing to be refused."* We have liberty, which we enjoy in Christ Jesus.

Everything we partake of is sanctified by the Word of God. By prayer and the Word of God, through faith all this is possible in Jesus.

We must also note the two-fold meaning here as well. This vision Peter saw was also one for the Gentiles. For now the gospel would be brought to them as well as the Jews (Acts 10:28; 10:34). *"God is not a respector of persons,"* salvation is to all who call upon Him.

"If thou put the brethren in remembrance of these things, thou shalt be a good minister of Je'sus Christ, nourished up in the words of faith and of good doctrine, whereunto thou hastattained."

4:6

It is the duty of all ministers to remind believers and instill within them the necessity to watch out for false teachers. If one is warned of their antics they'll be less able to be seduced by the Judaizing teachers or other false teachers.

These are good ministers of Jesus Christ, who are diligent in the ministry. Put the brethren in remembrance of what they have received and heard (2Pet. 1:12; 3:11).

All true men of God must put the church in remembrance of the Apostles' Doctrine. As our brother Jude declared *"I will therefore put you in remembrance,"* (Jude 5).

Every believer has a need to grow and increase in the knowledge of Jesus and His Word, His doctrine. The best way we help each other grow in grace, is to teach one another.

"But refuse profane and old wives' fables, and exercise thyself rather unto godliness."

"For bodily exercise profiteth little: but godliness is profitable unto all things, having promise of the life that now is, and of that which is to come."

4: 7-8

" Refuse profane and old wives' fables" Jewish traditions which people were filling their minds full of. Those who are godlymust *"exercise thyself rather*

unto godliness." The gain of godliness is far better than that of the law or
"profane fables." In the New Testament under grace we have greater
promises and hope in the eternal. The Old Testament promises were
temporal. Refuse the profane is not enough; we must exercise ourselves unto
godliness.

Abstaining from meats and marriages will not get you any closer to God.
What will it avail us to ratify the body, and not the sin? We must not only
cease to do evil, but learn to do well (Is. 1: 16-17). Paul says godliness is
"profitable for all things, having the promise of the life which now is."

"This is a faithful saying and worthy of all acceptation."

*"For therefore we both labour and suffer reproach, because we trust in the
living God, who is the Saviour of all men, specially of those that believe."*
4: 9-10

Here is another of Paul's "*faithful saying and worthy of all acceptation.*" As
men of God, ministers of the True Gospel of our Lord and Savior the
Apostles' Doctrine, we must labor and expect reproach, and persecution. Toil
and trouble are to be expected from the world. Yet, because we trust in the
living God, who is the Savior of all men, Jesus Christ, He will not only
provide for us, He will protect us as well. Our hope of a future resurrection is
far worth our troubles, persecutions, etc. Those who trust in Jesus shall never
be ashamed.

"These things command and teach."
*"Let no man despise thy youth; but be thou an example of the believers, in
word, in conversation, in charity, in spirit, in faith, in purity."*
"Till I come, give attendance to reading, to exhortation, to doctrine."
4: 11-13

"*These things command and teach.*" Be an example as a man of God (tupos)
means: "model, image, ideal, a pattern. A Pastor or anyone in a leadership
position within the church must be a model of faithfulness, holiness, love and
perseverance in godly living.

Paul was encouraging Timothy to read and exhort the Word of God, the
doctrine. He must not only teach them the doctrine, but what to believe as
well. Ministers must teach and command the things that they themselves
were taught and learned. *"Teaching them to observe all things whatsoever I
(Jesus) have commanded"* (Matt. 28:20).

As leaders (Elders, Bishops, Deacons etc.) we must practice what we preach. We are to be an ensample to the flock. We are to give ourselves to reading, to exhortation, to doctrine.

Paul's letters to Timothy were written to a young man who ventured out on his own in the midst of a confusing world full of pressures and challenges. Paul commanded Timothy to remain in Ephesus and lead the local church there (v. 1:3). Timothy found himself in a new place surrounded by new people who were falling prey to a slew of new (and false) doctrines. All of us today face a similar situation. Regardless of whether we spend most of our time in the classroom, the workplace, the home or even the market place, we are surrounded by strange ideas, opinions and philosophies that are competing for our attention. Many of which contradict the Word of God. What should we believe? How should we live?

We can divide the content of Paul's letters to Timothy into two categories, those things Paul commanded Timothy to teach (Timothy's ministerial role in the church) and instruction concerning the way in which Timothy was to live (Timothy's personal walk before others). Paul instructed him to watch his lifestyle and his doctrine (v.13). To paraphrase verse 16, Paul told Timothy, "Be careful and pay close attention to your belief and behavior." Timothy needed to be vigilant and serious about his belief and his behavior. What we believe determines how we act; and as those owned by another, we must be sure that our doctrine is correct and that our lifestyle is consistent with our doctrine. If we are truly living a life that glorifies God, we will follow Paul's instruction to Timothy, and God's instruction to us- Watch yourself! Do not be nonchalant about what you believe or how you live.

Paul instructs Timothy concerning how to live a life that honors God. How, exactly, are we to live a life that glorifies the Lord in a world of confusion, pressure and constant change?

First, we must lead by example (v.12). Be a person of integrity. Do not give others a reason to criticize your behavior or lifestyle. Lead by example in word (speech), conversation (conduct and lifestyle), charity (love), spirit (inward attitude), faith (what you believe) and purity (sexual chastity). Second, we must continue in the faith (vv. 13, 15-16). The "faith" entails the entire body of Christians doctrine revealed in the Word of God. To continue means one must first be grounded in the truth (2Tim. 1:5; 3:15); one must then refrain from moving from that which is true (1:18-19; 6: 20-21; 2Tim.

1:13-14); then one must grow in the knowledge of Christ, studying and meditating upon His Word (2Tim. 2:15; 3: 14-15). Third, we must minister to others (vv. 14-15). The Lord has gifted every believer for service in Christ's body (1Pet. 4: 10-11). We are to give ourselves "wholly" to that which God has called us to do. Half heartedness is never an option. Finally, we must abide by God's relationship standards (5:1-2). Treat your peers as part of your family. Remain pure; flee from any form of fornication. Living a life that honors God as outlined in this passage will cause us to be a testimony to the lost and to "save thyself" and them that hear thee" (v.16), that is, to receive deliverance from the bondage of sin and from the worlds corrupt influence.

"Neglect not the gift that is in thee, which was given thee by prophecy, with the laying on of the hands of the presbytery."
"Meditate upon these things; give thyself wholly to them; that thy profiting may appear to all."
"Take heed unto thyself, and unto the doctrine; continue in them: for in doing this thou shalt both save thyself, and them that hear thee."
4: 14-16

Whatever the gift Timothy had, Paul exhorts him not to neglect his gift which was given him from God by prophecy and with the laying on of hands by Paul.

Having been given this great work, Timothy must give himself wholly to them, that his profiting may appear to all. He was to meditate, on what? The doctrine of course, by doing so, they shall gain profit (i.e. in knowledge and grace).

Continue in the Apostles' Doctrine, live a holy life, (v. 12), teach sound doctrine, (vv13, 15-16), guarding the faith (6:20), and watching over ones spiritual life (v 16). These are essential for not only Timothy's salvation but for all of us.

As a minister, Pastor of a church, they must not fail to declare the full council of God, by faithfully warning and teaching the congregation (flock). A true shepherd must protect the flock from their enemies and protect them from paganistic ideas and theologies that will destroy their faith.

Paul called these false teachers "grievous wolves" (Acts 20:29). These were individuals who were drawing away the sheep from the teachings of Jesus and pointing them toward their distorted gospel. In doing this, "we shall be free from the blood of all men." If we neglect, we will be held accountable and their blood will be on our hands (Ez. 34: 1-10). In continuing the doctrine of Christ we shall save ourselves and them that hear us (Ez. 33:9).

"Rebuke not an elder, but intreat him as a father; and the younger men as brethren:"
"The elder women as mothers; the younger as sisters, with all purity."
5: 1-2

Be kindly affectionate to our elders. Respect must be placed upon them to their office in the church. The younger men, however, must be rebuked as brethren, with love and gentleness. Love and compassion must be evoked with the rebuke. The same respect is given to the women as well.

"Honour widows that are widows indeed."
"But if any widow have children or nephews, let them learn first to shew piety at home, and to requite their parents: for that is good and acceptable before God."

"Now she that is a widow indeed, and desolate, trusteth in God, and continueth in supplications and prayers night and day."
"But she that liveth in pleasure is dead while she liveth."
"And these things give in charge, that they may be blameless."
"But if any provide not for his own, and specially for those of his own house, he hath denied the faith, and is worse than an infidel."
"Let not a widow be taken into the number under threescore years old, having been the wife of one man,"

"Well reported of for good works; if she have br ought up children, if she have lodged strangers, if she have washed the saints' feet, if she have relieved the afflicted, if she have diligently followed every good work."

"But the younger widows refuse: for when they have begun to wax wanton against Christ, they will marry;"
"Having damnation, because they have cast off their first faith."

"And withal they learn to be idle, wandering about from house to house; and not only idle, but tattlers also and busybodies, speaking things which they ought not."

"I will therefore that the younger women marry, bear children, guide the house, give none occasion to the adversary to speak reproachfully."
"For some are already turned aside after Sa'tan."

"If any man or woman that believeth have widows, let them relieve them , and let not the church be charged; that they may relieve them that are widows indeed."

Honor is given unto the widows. We are to care for them. In the apostolic times widows had a great work in the church. They tended to the sick and aged (Acts 6:1). The church was to support the widows. The widows put their faith and trust in the Lord 100%. A good example of the office the widows attended to is found in Luke. Anna was a widow who *"departed not form the temple, but served God with fasting and prayer nightand day,"* (Luke 2:37). Anna never remarried, but dedicated herself to the Lord.

But the widow that liveth in the sin of the world " *is dead while she lives,"* (v 6). She is not a living member of the church, but a mortified member. Those, not only widows, but everyone who lives in pleasures are walking dead people; they are spiritually dead, dead in trespasses and sins.

Paul also states that if a widow has family alive let them take care of her and not burden the church (v 16). This is showing piety at home (v.4). Those who do not care for their own poor family members do in effect deny the faith, for the law of God says, *"Honour thy Father and Mother."*

If a widow has relieved the afflicted let her be relieved now. If she has lodged strangers, washed the saints feet, cared for the sick and aged (v. 10) let the church give unto her maintenance. However, the younger widows refuse: for they will grow weary with the work in the church. If let alone they'll remarry and cast off their first faith (v. 12).

When one has too much time on their hands they become idle and not only idle but tattlers. A busy-body sowing discord in the church (v. 13).
"Let the elders that rule well be counted worthy of double honour, especially they who labour in the word and doctrine."

"For the scripture saith, TOU SHALT NOT MUZZLE TE OX THAT TREADETH OUT THE CORN. And, The labourer is worthy of his reward."

The pastors and ministers who work hard in the Word and kingdom of God must receive double honor. We are speaking of the overseers of the local church who watch over the souls in their congregations. Who labour in word and doctrine?

These men who labor diligently in word and doctrine were worthy of double honor,esteemed and maintained. "Thou shall not muzzle the ox." The oxen were allowed to feed while they did the work. The more work they did, the more food they had.

Likewise, the Elders who labored were to be well provided f or. *"For the workman is worthy of his meat"* (Matt. 10:10; Luke 10:7; 1Cor. 9:7). God has always taken care of His ministers in the Old Testament and New Testament under the law and now under grace.

When an accusation is brought against an elder it must be accompanied by two or more credible witnesses (Deut. 19:15; Matt.18:16; Jn. 8:17; 2Cor.3:1). The accusation must be received before them. In other words the accused must face their accusers face to face.

"Them that sin rebuke before all, that others also may fear."
5:20

After two witnesses have brought an accusation and if found to be true, the elder who in "sin rebuke before all." The Bishops or other elders must not be silent about the sin of other elders. These elders must receive "rebuke" or be disciplined. His sin must be exposed "before all" (made public), so that the rest of the elders will experience the fear of God. This public rebuke is for the good of others.

"I charge thee before God, and the Lord Je'sus Christ, and the elect angels, that thou observe these things without preferring one before another, doing nothing by partiality."
5:21

"God is not a respector of persons," (Acts 10:34; 1Pet 1:17; Col. 3:25; Eph. 6:9). Therefore, His ministers must not show partiality either. Paul charged them before God, to guard against partiality.

The actual translation for this verse is: *"I charge thee in sight of God and Christ Jesus…"*
"Lay hands suddenly on no man, neither be partaker of other men's sins: keep thyself pure."
5:22

This verse is referring to the ordaining of men in the ministry. This is not to be done in haste. No one should be ordained unless they meet the qualifications as given by God (3: 1-7). Those who are to be ordained need to have a history of faithfulness to God, the church and ministry. The statement to "Keep thyself pure: means to refuse to become involved in the selection or ordination of anyone unworthy for the office of an elder (Acts 6:6; 2Tim. 1:6).

"Drink no longer water, but use a little wine for thy stomach's sake and thine often infirmities."
5:23

This verse is very conspicuous in that it shows that Timothy did not normally drink wine of any sort. Apparently, Paul had instructed him to drink a little wine for medicinal purposes, for a stomach ailment he had received from the alkali in the water. This wine was not fermented wine it was non-intoxicating.

The writer Athenaeums states, "Let him take sweet wine, either mixed with water or warmed, especially that kind called Protropes [juice coming from the grapes before they are pressed], as being good for the stomach, for sweet wine [orinos] does not make the head heavy" (Athenaeums, banquet, 2:24; see also Pliney Natural History 14.18).

"Some men's sins are open beforehand, going before to judgment; and some men they follow after."
"Likewise also the good works of some are manifest beforehand; and they that are otherwise cannot be hid."
5: 24-25

Some men's sins are so pellucid and obvious, that there is no controversy, no dispute. *"They go before to judgment,"* to lead them to censure, *"others follow after."* Their wickedness may not be manifest at the present time, or even after they are censured they continue in their sin.

There are hidden, secret sins, and there are open sins. The unconscionable cannot be hid, for God will bring to light the hidden things of darkness, and make manifest the sin within one heart.

Those who practice sin cannot inherit the Kingdom of God (Gal. 5:21). Therefore, one must resist sin and put to death the works of the flesh.

"Let as many servants as are under the yoke count their own masters worthy of all honour, that the name of God and his doctrine be not blasphemed."

"And they that have bel ieving masters, let them not despise them, because they are brethren; but rather do them service, because they are faithful and beloved, partakers of the benefit. These things teach and exhort."
6: 1-2

Paul elaborates on the duties of the servants. These servants were still "yoked" (zugos 2218) "submissive to authority." They are yoked to work, a bondservant to their master. Nevertheless, of their bondage, they are to respect their masters. "Count them worthy of all honor (Because they are their masters) respect, and obedience. In doing so the name of neither God nor His doctrine would be blasphemed (blasphemia 988) to make defamatory remarks of the Divine Majesty.

If servants become disobedient to their masters, (who are Christians) the doctrine ofJesus, the apostles' doctrine would be reflected upon them, as if they never had received the gospel. If ministers today, or any profess Christianity for that matter, behave themselves poorly the name of God and His doctrine are in danger of being blasphemed by those who seek to speak evil of His worthy name by which we are called (Jas. 2:7). This scripture applies to both master and servants. Because in Christ there is neither bond nor free.

Those with believing masters continue to do them service, because they are faithful and beloved. We all are partakers of the "Benefit", that is the benefit of being a Christian.

Believing masters and servants are brethren, in the same body, and partakers of the benefit, joint-heirs together in Christ Jesus.

"If any man teach otherwise, and consent not to wholesome words, even the words of our Lord Je'sus Christ, and to the doctrine which is according to godliness;"

"He is proud, knowing nothing, but doting about questions and strifes of words, whereof cometh envy, strife, railings, evil surmising,"
"Perverse disputing of men of corrupt minds, and destitute of the truth, supposing that gain is godliness: from such withdraw thyself."
6: 3-5

Any teaching that has not originated from Jesus or His apostles and does not carry the call for godliness and holiness is a different gospel then what the apostles' had brought. We are not supposed to submit to any other message, other than what Jesus has brought to us. The doctrine of our Lord and Savior is a doctrine according to godliness.

He who does not adhere to the true gospel of our Lord is proud (v. 4), contentious and ignorant, knowing nothing. But, run about with doting (noseo

3552) "to be ill, to be ailing." The primary meaning of "dote" is to be foolish (Jer. 50:36) "to be unsound"

Strife of words (eris 2054) "variance, contentions" whereof cometh…

Envy (perthonos 5355) "envy, jealousy" is the feeling of displeasure produced by witnessing or hearing of the advantage or prosperity of others, this evil sense always attaches to this word which will produce strife.

Railings (blasphemia 988) "Evil speaking" blasphemy.
Evil surmising (huponoea (huponoea 5282) "To suppose, conjecture, surmise," is translated "deemed" In other words to think under privately.

Perv erse disputing (diaparatribe 3859) "a constant or incessant wrangling" (dia, "through," para, "besides," tribo, "to wear out," suggesting the attrition or wearing effect of contention) "wrangling."

When men are no longer content with the words of Jesus, they surmise their own and impose them upon others. They sow these seeds of discord with man's wisdom not that which the Holy Spirit teaches, in doing so they sow discord in the church.

Men with corrupt minds have no solidity in them they are destitute of the truth. These, according to Paul were who Timothy was to withdraw from. Whoever does this, teach otherwise is proud, and knoweth nothing. Pride and ignorance run together.

When men leave the True Gospel of our Lord Jesus they will never agree with one another. But will perpetually fight, argue, and quarrel amongst themselves. Envy and strife will enter in the body. They become jealous and suspicious of each other. They will not only argue over manmade teachings but titles as well. "I'm an Elder, Apostle, or Prophet" etc. look at me. What I teach is equal with Jesus' doctrine they say in their hearts. They try to make a name for themselves instead of lifting up the only saving name, Jesus! We are told to separate from these individuals

"come out from among them, my people, and be ye separate," says the Lord (Rev. 18:4).

Again, anything contrary or any extra biblical doctrine is unapostolic and ignores the pellucid admonitions in this epistle as well as others (Gal. 1:9).

"But godliness with contentment is great gain."
"For we brought nothing into this world, and it is certain we can carry

nothing out."
"And having food and raiment let us be therewith content."
"But they that will be rich fall into temptation and a snare, and into many foolish and hurtful lusts, which drown men in destruction and perdition."

"For the love of money is the root of all evil: which while some coveted after, they have erred from the faith, and pierced themselves through with many sorrows."

6: 6-10

"Godliness with contentment is great gain." False teachers will portray to be a holy, righteous man just to gain monetarily. These prosperity preachers are driven by motivation of greed and self gain. They teach their congregation that their wealth is a sighof God's approval.

Where there is true godliness there will be true contentment and great gain. All true men of God (and women) have learned like Paul to be content in whatever state they find themselves (Phil. 4:11). They are content to whatever God has blessed them with. Verse 7 explains our reasoning for such contentment. We came into the world with nothing, yet our Lord had provided for us, even if we lose everything we have, we can be no poorer than when we came into this world (Job 1:21).

If God has provided for us the necessities of life we need to be content with this. We don't need fancy cars, homes, jewelry and clothes. This was Agar's prayer (Prov. 30:8).

Notice verse 9 it does not say those who are rich, but those that will be rich. Those that place their happiness in worldly covetness fall into temptation and a snare. For when the enemy (devil) sees that you are lusting after the things of the flesh he will lay and wait for you, waiting to entrap you. Like a bird that is snared, doesn't even know that it is to take his life (Prov. 7:23; Ecc.9:12). These worldly lusts *"will drown men in destruction and perdition."*

Destruction (olethros 3629) "ruin" The indulgence of the flesh will bring about aphysical "ruin," and possibly that of the whole being.
Perdition (apollumi 622) "to destroy utterly," "to perish."

Money is not evil, nor for one to have it is a sin. But "the love of money is the root of all evil…" While men covet after and lust after money, they neglect the things of God, and "pierced themselves through with many sorrows." Covetous people will give up on Jesus, if necessary to get money (2Tim. 4:10). For the world, the things of the world are more important to them than the things of God.

"But thou, O man of God, flee these things; and follow after righteousness, godliness, faith, love, patience, meekness."
6:11

After these warnings and exhortation Paul calls Timothy a "man of God." Men of God ought to conduct themselves as becometh a Christian, walk circumspectly. Paul told Timothy to flee from these things mentioned in the previous verses. Men of God need to keep their eyes on the heavenly not the things of the earth.

To arm himself against the lust of the flesh, Paul directs Timothy to follow that of the spirit which is good. Follow after:
Righteousness (dikaiosune 1343) is "the character or quality of being right or just"

Godliness (eusekeia 2150) from eu, "well and sebomai, "to be devout," denotes that piety which, characterized by a God ward attitude.
Faith (pistis 4102) primarily, "firm persuasion," always of "faith in God or Christ, or things spiritual.
Love (agape 26) "affection or benevolence" "charity"
Patience (hupomone 5281) "an abiding under: (hupo, "under," meno, "to abide"), patience, which grows only in trials
Meekness (praupathia 4236) "Gentleness" humility
Righteousness: in his conversation toward men
Godliness: toward God
Faith and Love: as living principles
Patience: to bear the rebukes and reproaches of men
Meekness: to instruct the gainsayers
These are the things men of God must follow after. In doing so they would not be so tempted to follow after the things of the world.
"Fight the good fight of faith, lay hold on eternal life, whereunto thou art also called, and hast professed a good profession before many witnesses."
6:12

Paul exhorts Timothy to do his part as a soldier of Christ. *"Fight the good fight of faith."* Fight (agonizomai 75) "to contend" perseveringly against opposition and temptation. Paul views a Christian life as a fight. It's an intense struggle that requires persevering in the things of God and contending with the adversaries of the truth. All of us are called to "contend for the faith which was once delivered unto the saints" (Jude 3).

It's a fight of faith, and the weepers of our warfare are not carnal… (2Cor. 10: 3-4). The only weapons adequate enough to destroy the works of the enemy are those which God gives us. Paul listed some of these weapons in verse 11.

" *Lay hold on eternal life*" Eternal life is the crown of life proposed to us if we endure to the end, this is to encourage us to war, "*fight the good fight of faith*" "*Hold fast that which thou hast, that no man take thy crown*" (Rev 3:11)

All true men of God make a good profession before one and all, confession by acknowledgment of the truth.

Perhaps one of the most difficult concepts for a new believer to understand is that receiving Jesus does not guarantee a life free from trouble. Do not misunderstand are who in Christ is "a new creature (2Cor. 5:17), born into the family of God (Jn. 1:12). He has been redeemed, justified, reconciled and sanctified. Yet, it sometimes comes as quite a shock that while we are still in our earthly bodies we will experience physical, emotional, interpersonal and even spiritual battles at times. New Christians are sometimes given the wrong impression: "Trust Christ, and all your troubles will be gone," but that thinking flies in the face of truths presented in scripture (Jn. 16:33). Paul later told Timothy, "*yea, and all that will live Godly in Christ Jesus shall suffer persecution*" (2Tim. 3:12).

The Word of God uses the language of warfare (2Tim. 2:3) and of athletic contests (2Tim. 2:5) to prepare our minds and hearts for the fact that we have entered into a tremendous struggle with the forces of evil (Eph.6:12). We face a constant battle against the flesh (Gal. 5:17), the devil (1Pet.5:8) and a fallen world that loves sin and error and hates truth devil (1Pet.5:8) and a fallen world that loves sin and error and hates truth 21). Thus, Paul calls Timothy to "fight a good fight" against the enemy around him. Late, the apostles own triumphant epitaph reads, "I have fought a good fight," (2Tim. 4:7). A battle is raging and God exhorts you to the part of a soldier. You must "endure hardness, as a soldier of Jesus Christ (2Tim. 2:3). Believers must contend against corruption and temptations and oppose the powers of darkness.

"I give thee charge in the sight of God, who quickeneth all things, and before

Christ Je'sus, who before Pon'ti-us Pi'late witnessed a good confession;"
6:13

God the Father quickens (gives life to) the dead (rom. 4:17). Yet we know the spirit will do so (Rom. 8:11). They are the same.

Paul charges (parangello 3853) "To announce beside" (para, "beside" angello "to announce") "to hand out an announcement from one to another," usually denotes "to command, to charge."

Paul commanded Timothy before Jesus, to whom in a particular manner he stood related as a minister of the gospel. "Who before Pontius Pilate witnessed a good confession; *"That I should bear witness of the truth. Everyone that is of the truth heareth my voice,"* (Jn. 18: 36-37). The good confession of Jesus was *"my kingdom is not of this world."* Paul reminds Timothy of his own profession in v.12 when he was ordained and to be quickened by this and to fulfill his duty in the ministry.

"That thou keep this commandment without spot, unrebukeable, until the appearing of our Lord Je'sus Christ:"
6:14

And Timothy "keep this commandment" as long as you shall live (until Jesus comes back). Without spot (aspilo 784) "unspotted, unstained" keeping a commandment without alteration and in the fulfillment of it.

Unrebukeable (anepilestos 4230 "that cannotbe laid hold," hence, "not open to censure, irreproachable."

Ministers should be looking for the blessed hope of our Lord's second coming. They are to keep this commandment without alteration and irreproachable. Of course no one knows the time or season Jesus will return, however we are encouraged to look for His return any day.

"Which in his times he shall shew, who is the blessed and only Potentate, the King of kings, and Lord of lords;"

"Who only hath immortality, dwelling in the light which no man can approach unto; whom no man hath seen, nor can see: to whom be honour and power everlasting. Amen"

6: 15-16

Of course we know Jesus is coming back to the Mount of Olives as King of kings and Lord of lords to war against the nations (Acts 1: 9-12; Rev. 19: 11-

16).

Paul states that Jesus is the blessed and only Potentate One. He has all power in heaven and in the earth (Matt. 28:18). All the kings of the earth are placed in position by Jesus, He gives them their power. He has sovereign dominion over them. On Jesus' vesture is written King of Kings and Lord of Lords (Rev. 19:16) His name is higher than any name. Only He has mortality.

Not only has no human ever seen God, but no human can see God. God the Spirit is invisible (Col. 1:15; Heb. 11:27; 1Tim. 1:7) In the Old Testament God manifested Himself many times in visible ways (Gen. 18:1; Ex. 33: 22-23). These temporary, visible manifestations are called theophanies. In the New Testament God manifested Himself in human flesh as Jesus Christ, the Son of God (Jn. 1:1; 14; 1Tim. 3:16). Jesus is the Son of God- God in the flesh (Matt. 1:21-23). He has a dual nature, human and divine, or flesh and spirit. In His humanity He is the Son of Mary, however, at the same time Jesus is the One God Himself (2Cor. 5:19; Col. 2:9; 1Tim. 3:16). Jesus is God manifested in flesh (Isa. 9:6; Jn. 10:30; 14:6-11), Yahweh or Jehovah (Jer. 23:6), the Word (Jn. 1:14), the Holy Spirit (2Cor 3:17; Gal. 4:6; Eph. 3:16-17).

Jesus is the name of the Father, Son, and Holy Ghost, for Jesus is the revealed name of God in the New Testament (Jn. 5:43; Matt. 1:21; Jn. 14:26). That's why baptism in His name is correct and proper (Acts 2:38).

In essence, all of God is in Jesus and we find all we need in Him. The only God we will ever see in heaven is Jesus. He is Yahweh of the Old Testament (Jn. 8:24). To Him *"be honour and power everlasting."*Amen.

"Charge them that are rich in this world, that they be not highminded, nor trust in uncertain riches, but in the living God, who giveth us richly all things to enjoy;"

"That they do good, that they be rich in good works, ready to distribute, willing to communicate;"
6:17-18

Paul commanded Timothy to charge the rich to beware of temptations. Not to be high-minded, lifted up with pride. This is a sin that easily over takes a rich person. Charge them not to be boastful, puffed up, prideful, because of their wealth. Charge them to trust in God not the arm of the flesh.

To do good with what God has blessed them with. " *That they be rich in good works, ready to distribute, willing to communicate."* Not only to help and give to others, but do it willingly. God loves a cheerful giver.

Ministers must not be afraid to speak against the prideful, and to stir them up to do good works of piety and charity. In doing so *"they may lay hold on eternal life."*

"O Tim'o-thy, keep that which is committed to thy trust, avoiding profane and vainbabblings, and oppositions of science falsely so called:"
"Which some professing have erred concerning the faith. Grace be with thee. Amen."

Once again Paul is reminding Timothy to guard the faith that has been entrusted to him. The literal Greek rendition means "keep the deposit" and refers to an obligation of keeping safe a treasured possession committed to one's care. The true Gospel of our Lord Jesus Christ has been entrusted to us by the Holy Spirit. We must proclaim it and be ready to defend it against false teachers.

Ministers are to *" avoid vain babblings and oppositions of science."* Those who adhere to these things are in danger of erring concerning the truth, and leaving it.

Paul concludes his epistle with a solemn prayer, *"Grace be with you."* God will not withhold anything good from His children. God will give grace and glory to all who walk upright. Grace be with you all. Amen.

Introduction to 2nd Timothy

This second epistle Paul wrote to Timothy from Rome. The emperor Nero was trying to stop the spread of Christianity in Rome. Therefore, he had Paul imprisoned once again. Paul suffered as any common criminal would. He was deserted at the end of his ministry by his friends.

Paul writes to Timothy as a beloved son and faithful co-worker. Because of his closeness with Timothy he entrusted him with the delivery of six of his epistles. As Paul faced the prospect of execution, he petitions Timothy twice to join him in Rome again. Timothy was still at Ephesus when Paul wrote this epistle.

Paul wrote this second epistle to exhort Timothy to guard the gospel, preach the Word, and to fulfill his charge. Knowing he would face hardship and persecution from within the church.

This is the last recorded words of Paul before his execution by Nero. Almost 35 years after his conversion to Jesus on the Road of Damascus. This epistle contains one of the most perspicuous statements in the Bible about divine inspiration. Paul encourages us (believers) to be committed to God's Word and be ready to teach others. The recurring themes throughout are to hold fast to the faith (Jesus and the original apostolic gospel), and to guard it against polluters, false teachers. This epistle differs somewhat from the previous one. The former related to Timothy's office as an evangelist this one more of personal conduct and behavior.

"Paul, an apostle of Je'sus Christ by the will of God, according to the promise of life which is in Christ Je'sus,"
"To Tim'o-thy, my dearly beloved son: Grace, mercy, and peace, from God the Father and Christ Je'sus our Lord."

Paul has bestowed upon himself the title "apostle" of Jesus Christ. Not appointed by man, but God. He was called, appointed and anointed by God. It was by the ordained will of God, "According to the promise of life which is in Christ Jesus," according to the Gospel. The gospel is the promise life of Jesus. Jesus is the Way, the Truth, and the Life (Jn. 14:6).

Paul calls Tim othy his beloved "beloved son" this shows the love and compassion he felt toward him. Also, Paul did not receive the gospel from man, ho man taught him. It was given to him by Jesus (Gal. 1:12).

The general context of the salutations themselves shows that Paul emphasizes two different manifestations of God, and all these New Testament greetings focus on the two roles of God as Father and Son. When one reads the remarks immediately after the salutations it is obvious that the writer, in the context of the greeting was praising and glorifying what God has done in Jesus as the Son.

"I thank God, whom I serve from my forefathers with pure conscience, that without ceasing I have remembrance of thee in my prayers night and day;"

1:3

Paul's thanksgiving for Timothy to God was that he remembered him in prayer. For whatever we do for the furtherance of the gospel we must thank God for it. It is God who puts in our heart to remember such things as prayer for our brethren. Paul remembered Timothy in his prayers night and day, he did this without ceasing.

Paul served God from his forefathers. He had kept a pure conscience, one without offence (Acts 24:16).

"Greatly desiring to see thee, being mindful of thy tears, that I may be filled with joy;"
"When I call to remembrance the unfeigned faith that is in thee, which dwelt first in thy grandmother Lo'is, and thy mother Eu'nice; and I am

persuaded that in thee also."
1: 4-5

Timothy was sorrowful when he left Paul and went away tearfully. Paul knowing death was imminent desired to see him once again. He begs him to remain faithful to the truth of the gospel and hurry to come and see him. Timothy had a good grand-mother and mother they were faithful, though his father did not believe (Acts 16:1). Paul had great hope for Timothy, for he had *"no man like minded"* (Phil. 2:20) *"of equal soul."*

Like Paul we are to remember our friends and loved ones in our prayers without ceasing. We should rejoice when we see our brothers and sisters walking in the truth (2Jn. 4).

"Wherefore I put thee in remembrance that thou stir up the gift of God, which is in thee by the putting on of my hands."
"For God hath not given us the spirit of fear; but of power, and of love, and of a sound mind."
1: 6-7

There fore, it is needful to remind you Timothy to stir up the "gift" (GK Charisma) of God. The gift given to Timothy is composed of fire (1Thess. 5:19), therefore, he must stir or fan this into flames. These gifts are given to us by the Holy Spirit. We fan or stir this up with our diligence, obedience, faith and prayer through the grace of God. To quench the spirit is to put the fire out (1Thess. 5:19).

Timothy must take every opportunity to use these gifts given him, in doing so stir them up; this is how he could increase them. Use the gifts and have gifts. We know Timothy had the Holy Ghost what other gifts he had we do not know. However, out of fear many will not use their gifts. Therefore, Paul tells him that God had not *"given us the spirit of fear,"* but,He gave us his Spirit which imparts "power, love, and a sound mind." He's given us the power to face adversities, the spirit of love to God, and the spirit of a gentle, peaceful mind. What we receive from God is not fearful, but a courageous spirit, power to speak His name, power to heal, power to witness, power to speak the words of truth.

"Be not thou therefore ashamed of the testimony of our Lord, nor of me his prisoner: but be thou partaker of the afflictions of the gospel according to the power of God;"

1:8

Don't be ashamed of the gospel of Jesus Christ nor of me (Paul) His prisoner. We must not be ashamed of those who suffer for the gospel. The gospel is the testimony of Jesus.

Paul was a prisoner of Jesus Christ (Eph. 4:1). It was for Jesus' sake he was imprisoned in Nero's prison. We are not to only sympathize with those who suffer for Jesus, but we suffer with them. As men of God, we must expect afflictions and persecution for the gospel sake. Jesus still suffers with us as we carry the gospel to the lost everywhere (Col. 1:24; Acts 9:4).

We live in troublesome times, concerning the days before the coming of our Lord in the air, the bible speaks of perilous days, deceptive days, days in which, *"all that will live in Godly in Christ Jesus shall suffer persecution"* (3:12). We must admit that we are, at times, fearful; we still possess the old nature and can be overtaken with the cares and fears of life. However, when we do worry and fear, we forego peace, joy and confidence in service. We want to look into the bible to find God's will regarding this important matter of "fear." In the King James Version Bible, three underlying Greek words are translated "fear" or one of its synonyms. While in every instance the translation is correct, it is instructive to consider the shades of difference in the meanings of the underlying Greek words and to see how the context of the English word invariably reveals that same distinction in meaning.
The Bible always uses the Greek word for fear, deilia, in a negative sense. It is the fear, fright or cowardice that stems from a reaction of the flesh to a frightening situation. For example, the unsaved, the "fearful…shall have their part" in the lake of fire (Rev. 21:8). Their fear is certainly understandable! In another passage we find that God has not given the believer "the spirit of fear: (v.7). The context reveals why this kind of fear needed to be rebuked (v.8). Some were cowering in the face of opposition to the faith; they feared being identified with a godly testimony. The Lord promises us the strength,

the overcoming love and the spirit-controlled mind to dispel this sinful emotion. This kind of fear is of the flesh, not the spirit.

"Who hath saved us, and called us with an holy calling, not according to our works, but according to his own purpose and grace, which was given us in Chris Je'sus before the world began,"

1:9

It is our faith in the gospel which has saved us. Therefore, we must not think much to suffer for it. Our salvation will be complete when Jesus comes back for His church, one without spot or blemish.

Jesus has called us, with a holy calling, which we are to labour in. We were not called because of our works (i.e. in keeping of the law) "but according to his purpose and grace." God's grace was given us before the world began. The gospel is the manifestation of this purpose and grace. The purpose of God was to destroy the works of the enemy, save us and abolish death. Jesus hath brought life and immortality to light by His gospel.

"Whereunto I am appointed a preacher, and an apostle, and a teacher of the Gen'tiles."

"For the which cause I also suffer these things: nevertheless I am not ashamed: for I know whom I have believed, and am persuaded that he is able to keep that which I have committed unto him against that day." "Hold fast the form of sound words, which thou hast heard of me, in faith and love whichis in Christ Je'sus."

1: 11-13

Paul was appointed to preach the Word of God to the Gentiles. He believed his calling appointment was worth suffering for. None of us should be ashamed to suffer for the gospel. Those who are in Jesus, and trust in Him, know Him, are acquainted with Him, and know He is worth the suffering.

Paul was entrusted with the Gospel of Jesus Christ, Therefore, as he was called to teach and preach he could boldly declare "To keep that which I have committed."

"Hold fast…sound words." The "sound words" Paul exhorted Timothy to hold on to were the original apostolic teachings, the doctrines which he had taught him. Timothy must hold to the doctrines of Jesus Christ "in faith and in love." He was to never depart or compromise these teachings. Regardless of it meant he would have to suffer, be rejected, or despised because of it (1Tim. 1:10; 6:3; Tit. 1:9; 13; 2:1-2, 8).

"That good thing which was committed unto thee keep by the Ho'ly Ghost which dwelleth in us."
1:14

We are to keep the doctrine within us by the power of the Holy Ghost. We are the Temple of the Living God. His Spirit dwells in us. It is this power which enables us to keep the pure unaltered gospel. We must guard, protect, and defend it. This is an essential duty of the men of God, to ensure not only salvation for those that hear us but for ourselves (3: 14-15; 1Tim. 4:16). As Jude exhorted *"contend for the faith,"* (3) means we struggle, suffer or fight for the truth. We remain faithful to the faith which was delivered by the apostles.

"This thou knowest, that all they which are in A'sia be turned away from me; of whom are Phygel'lus and Hermog'e-nes."
"The Lord give mercy unto the house of On-esiph'o-rus; for he oft refreshed me, and was not ashamed of my chain:"
"But, when he was in Rome, he sought me out very diligently, and found me."

"The Lord grant unto him that he may find mercy of the Lord in that day: and in how many things he ministered unto me at Eph'e-sus, thou knowest very well."

1: 15-18

All…turned away from me, here Paul sits in a Roman prison. The gospel of Jesus Christ, the one he has suffered greatly for was being persecuted. Yet, Paul remained faithful to God and His calling. He knew in his heart that the gospel would be preserved through servants such as Timothy.

Onesipnorus name appears only one other time in Scripture when the apostle Paul again mentions his household later in this epistle (4:19). Gut the few statements given concerning this man are fraught with meaning.

Through Paul, the Holy Spirit encouraged Timothy to hold fast to the Word of God (v.13) and to do so in the power of the spirit (v.14). He was to remain firm despite the fact that many had turned away (v.15). Rather than being tripped up by those who had shown themselves unfaithful, Timothy was to follow the example of those who had proven faithful, men such as Paul (vv8, 12) and Onesiphorus (vv. 16-180. The outstanding quality of Onesiphorus

was his merciful spirit and the refreshment that it brought to others; how much this meant to the apostle is indicated in the resounding tenderness in which he addressed this man and his household (vv16, 18). These verses give every evidence that Onesiphorus dearly loved Paul and sought him out when he heard that the apostle had been imprisoned in Rome (v. 17).
Mercy is the reward for those who have been merciful (Matt. 5:7), and

Paul prays diligently that "the Lord (would) give mercy unto the house of Onesiphorus" (v.16). Here the Bible gives us a dynamic example of a courageous man who committed himself to helping people even if it endangered his own life.

As we continue to remain steadfast and unmovable on the gospel we too can expect persecution. And will find ourselves abandoned like Paul had. Even with this dissention Paul had a faithful brother in Onesiphorus. He refreshed and encouraged Paul. He was not ashamed of Paul even though he was in prison. Notice Onesiphorus sought Paul out; and he found him. He ministered to Paul numerous times. We should always search out opportunities to do well to others. To help, pray for and encourage them.

Often in Scripture, we can learn a great deal about an individual from his name. The name Onesiphorus (v.16) means "help-bringer" or "profit-bearer." It comes from two words meaning "load" (actually used concerning tax assessment on a person or property) and "to gratify, have joy." Thus, we might say that Onesiphorus was a man who brought "a load of joy" to the apostle Paul.

True to his name, this man cast any consequences to the wind, boldly exposed himself to danger by visiting Paul in prison and encouraged him exposed himself to danger by visiting Paul in prison and encouraged him 17) he "refreshed" Paul. We are not told exactly how he refreshed him; perhaps he was able to bring food and clothing to that damp, dark Roman dungeon. But it would appear that the refreshment was more than just material. It was emphatically spiritual
– soul refreshment. The root of the word from which refreshed is translated is the word for "soul," and it means "to cool off, relieve, refresh, to recover from the effects of the heat." The visits from Onesiphorus encouraged and comforted Paul, probably in the sharing of Scripture and of prayer, and "cooled off his soul." Onesiphorus refreshed Paul not once or twice but many times. While others may have recoiled from Paul's chains, Onesiphorus was

not ashamed to Paul in prison (v. 16). In fact, standing alongside Paul as a friend and fellow believer was nothing new to this dear saint (v.18). He had in many ways and at numerous times provided for Paul at Ephesus. He lived a life of help and encouragement to others (Heb. 6:10).

Paul shows his appreciation by offering prayers on his behalf. "The Lord givesmercy unto the house of Onesiphorus." It's quite possible that Onesiphorus was present with Paul; this was why he prayed for his household in his absence (v.16).

Paul also prayed that Onesiphorus would find mercy in the day of the Lord. "Inthat day" refers to the Day of Judgment, we will be held accountable for what we done here on earth (2Cor. 5:10). We all should look for mercy of our Lord in that day (Jude 21).

"Thou therefore, my son, be strong in the grace that is in Christ Je'sus."
"And the things that thou hast heard of me among many witnesses, the same commit thou to faithful men, who shall be ableto teach others also."
2: 1-2

Paul encourages Timothy "to be strong in the grace" of Jesus, to be consistent and persevere regardless of what is taking place around him. As we go through adversities we have a necessity to grow stronger in Jesus (Eph. 6:10). His grace is more than sufficient for us. Grace and truth came by Jesus (Jn. 1:17) it is life, whereas the law came by Moses (death).

Now that Paul had taught Timothy he commands him to teach others. Train them in the ministry, commit to them the same things I which you learned from me. It's not that we must learn the truth for ourselves, but we must be apt to teach others.

"Thou therefore endure hardness, as a good soldier of Je'sus Christ."
"No man that warreth entangleth himself with the affairs of this life; that he may please him who hath chosen him to be a soldier."

A man of God who is committed to the gospel must "endure hardness, as a good soldier of Jesus Christ." We are to fight against the enemies of the Truth and defend it against compromise. Jesus is our captain (Heb.2:10). We are more than conquerors in Christ Jesus (Rom. 8:37). *"Greater is He* (Jesus) *that is in us, than he* (Satan) *that is in the world,"* (1Jn. 4:4). We are victorious and shall overcome through Him (1Cor. 15:57). As a soldier of Jesus, we must be willing to go through difficulties, trials, tribulation and persecution and to wage a spiritual warfare for our Lord to defend His gospel. In order for us to battle we must let go of all our heavy weights of the world. *"No man that warreth entangleth himself with the affairs of this life."* The way to please our Lord is to separate ourselves from the world.

We are exhorted to love not the world or the things in the world. The world and the true church of Jesus Christ are two distinct and opposite class of people. The world under the dominion of Satan, the church belongs to Jesus Christ. We overcome the affairs of this life (world) when we are born again in the Water and the Spirit (Jn. 3: 3-5; Acts 2:38; 1Jn. 5:4).

"And if a man also strive for masteries, yet is he not crowned, except he strive lawfully."
2:5
Masteries (gheb-oo naiv Heb. 1369) valor, victory: force, mastery, might, mighty (act, power), power, strength.
A believer must strive (athleo) a contest contend.
"And if anyone enters competitive
Games, he is not crowned unless he
Competes lawfully (fairly, according
To the rules laid down.")
Amplified

We cannot expect a prize unless we play fairly according to the rules set forth. We must therefore aim at mastering our own lusts and corruptions. If and when we play by the laws we shall obtain a crown after and only then can complete victory be obtained. We shall receive our reward of the glory and honor given to us by God.

"The husbandman that laboureth must be first partaker of the fruits."
"Consider what I say; and the Lord give thee understanding in all things."
2: 6-7
If we are to be first partaker of the fruit, we must labor for it. If we are to obtain a prize, we must run the race, we must labor with patience.

Paul admonishes Timothy to consider what he was telling him and he also prayed that God would give him understanding in all things. We must exhort and encourage those who hear us to consider what we say or teach. All spiritual understanding comes from God. He will teach us all things.

"Remember that Je'sus Christ of the seed of Da'vid was raised from the dead according to my gospel:"

"Wherein I suffer trouble, as an evildoer, even unto bonds; but the word of God is not bound."

"Therefore I endure all things for the elect's sakes, that they may also obtain thesalvation which is in Christ Je'sus with eternal glory."

"It is a faithful saying: For if we be dead with him, we shall also live with him:"

"If we suffer, we shall also reign with him: if we deny him, he also will deny us:"

"If we believe not, yet he abideth faithful: he cannot deny himself."

To offer an encouraging word to Timothy, Paul reminded him of the resurrection of Jesus. We are to look to Jesus, who is the author and finisher of our faith (Heb. 12:2).

Paul was a faithful servant of Jesus Christ, who done well. Yet he suffered "as an evildoer." However, he did not relent, sidestep nor neglect his holy vocation. He had assurance in the word and pressed forward. For he knew, although he was bond, God's word was not. Man may stop him, but not God's Word. It would go out and not return void. The power of God's word can never be rendered obsolete or void.

Paul suffered as an evildoer because of the Word of God. Though he was bond, God's word is never bound. He suffered with elation in his heart. Why?

"For the elects' sakes that they may also obtain the salvation," Although we suffer for our own salvation we should be willing to suffer for the souls of others as well. The elect (ekletos 1588) "chosen ones" the believers, both Jews and Gentiles alike are chosen to obtain salvation. This salvation is in Jesus. *There is no other name whereby we must be saved* (Acts 4:12).

Those who faithfully dedicated their lives to Jesus and followed His teachings, regardless the cost would reap great rewards. "If we be dead with him, we shall live with him." If we die to this world we shall live in a glorious better place with Him.

If we suffer (hupomeno 5278) "Endure or persevere." Those who remain steadfast in the faith to the end shall live and rule and reign with Jesus (Rev. 20:4). "If we deny Jesus, He will deny us on the day of judgment. If we deny Him before man, He will deny us before the Father (Matt. 10:33). This is the crux of the matter, whether we believe it or not. If we are faithful to Jesus, He will be faithful to us. *"For there is not one promise, one jot or tittle shall fall to the ground"* (Matt.5:18; Luke 16:17). His promises are yea and Amen. We shall sit upon the throne with Him, if we endure to the end (Matt. 19:28). He also issues a solemn warning to all who depart from His Word, from the faith (Titus 1:2; Rev. 3:7).

"Of these things put them in remembrance, charging them before the Lord that they strive not about words to no profit, but to the subverting of the hearers."

2:14

As men of God we are to edify those in the church, to continue to remind them of the things they do know and that they strive not about words "to no profit."

Subverting (catastrophe 2692) "an overthrow" of faith. Basically, Paul was telling Timothy to avoid petty controversy over words, which do no one any good. They create schisms, contentions upsets and undermines the faith of the hearers, which draws them away from the things of God. We, as men of God, must charge, bear witness, and encourage our fellow believers to avoid arguing and debating over the Word of God. Nothing positive will come out of this, only heartache, pain and anguish.

"Study to shew thyself approved unto God, a workman that needeth not to be ashamed, rightly dividing the word of truth." "But shun profane and vain babblings: for they will increase unto more ungodliness."
"And their word will eat as doth a canker: of whom is Hy-menae'us and Phile'tus;"
2: 15-17

If your ultimate goal is to please the Lord, then you need to heed these scriptures. The word study (spoudoza 4704) "to hasten to a thing, to exert oneself, endeavor, and givediligence." God's Word commands us to do this. Why? Just as in Timothy's day even a blameless preacher will find himself having to face critics and defend his position. As he, therefore, expounds the Word, whether those that hear him believe it or not, he knows he has faithfully discharged his duty as a man of God, *"approved unto God"* and who *"needs not to be ashamed."* Just like the prophets of old, he is cognizant that he has proclaimed the *"thus saith the Lord"* for today. He understands that the rejection or acceptance of God's messenger depends upon the listeners' response to the heavenly message.

To rightly divide the Word of God is not to reinvent it, but rightly divide the gospel that is committed to our trust. Don't add or take away from it. Timothy as well as any child of God must study God's Word diligently in order to"rightly divide."

Anything outside of God's Word, the teachings of Jesus and His apostles are considered *"profane and vain babblings"* which we are exhorted to avoid. These false teachings "will eat as a canker, or gangrene, when one becomes infected with their teaching if not stopped, will spread throughout the body.

Paul mentions two of these false teachers by name and warns people not to follow after their pernicious ways.
"Who concerning the truth have erred, saying that the resurrection is past already; and overthrow the faith of some."

"Nevertheless the foundation of God standeth sure, having this seal. The Lord knoweth them that are his. And, Let every one that nameth the name of Christ depart from iniquity."

"But in a great house there are not only vessels of gold and of silver, but also of wood and of earth; and some to honour, and some to dishonour."
2: 18-20

Many today within our churches profess to know Jesus but do not truly possess Him. Some even as Hymenaeus and Philetus pose as ministers of the Gospel, while denying the cardinal truths of the message they claim to preach. They may not be easy to spot, however, because they "privily… bring in damnable heresies" (2Pet. 2:1) to the detriment of the spiritual wellbeing of God's people. It is vital that those who desire to please God and obey His Word take a biblical stand by departing from iniquity and warning others of these divisive Charlatans.

Hyneneaeus and Philetus denied one of the very cornerstones of our faith – the Resurrection. Their sin was teaching error. Their influence in the church was so damaging that their words began to *"eat as doth a canker"* (v.17) so that they*"overthrew the faith of some."* (v.18). This defection could have shaken Timothy's confidence, so Paul gave him assurance and an authoritative command.

Regardless what these Charlatans false teachers do or say " *the foundation of God standeth sure, having the seal, The Lord knoweth them that are his"* (v.19). And what is the command that accompanies this blessed promise?
"Let every one that nameth the name of Christ depart from iniquity" (v. 19; 1

Tim.6: 3-5, 11). All who choose to ignore this divine injunction will surely fall prey to the enemies' devices and deceptions.

"But in a great house there are not only vessels of gold and of silver, but also of wood and of earth; and some to honour, and some to dishonour."

"If a man therefore purge himself from these, he shall be a vessel unto honour, sanctified, and meet for the master's use, and prepared unto every good work."

2: 20-21

In the church body of Jesus Christ is "a great house." This house is thoroughly furnished with expensive furniture and some inexpensive. "Vessels of gold and silver, but also of wood and of earth," the gold and silver are vessels of honor (wheat) meet for the master's use. The vessels of wood and earth, vessels of dishonour (tares). Some honour the church by teaching the true gospel of Jesus Christ, and some dishonour the church by their corrupt, profane, damnable heresies (false teachings). If the tree is good the fruit will be good as well. The necessity of sanctification from the world and unto God must take place in our life.

There are wheat (sons of God) and tares (son's of the evil one) in the same field, the body of Christ, the church. The vessels of honour will be beside the vessels of dishonour, and they will co-exist together until Jesus comes back. Then a separation will take place. Remember the Lord knows them who are His (v.19).

If a man purge himself from the mundane, the false teachers, he shall be a vessel of honor, one who is sanctified and meet for the master's use. *"Flee also youthful lusts: but follow righteousness, faith, charity, peace, with them that call on the Lord out of a pure heart."* 2:22

Though Timoth y was a holy man of God, Paul exhorts him to *"flee youthful lusts"* to keep himself pure from them. The lust of the flesh (Gal. 5: 19-21) are the youthful lusts one must flee from. Before our conversion we done these things, but now, these should not be part of our daily lives. Paul gives us an excellent remedy against youthful lust.

" Follow righteousness, faith, charity, peace," the more we draw closer to the things of God, the further we are from the lusts of the flesh. Being a child of God sets us apart from the world. We no longer indulge in the things of the world. We have a new home now, which is with Jesus. Therefore, because we

are now part of a new family, we must abstain from the evil pleasures of the world (1Pet. 2:11). Holy love and devotion to the things of God will cure impure lust.

" Follow peace with them that call on the Lord," (v.22), keeping a righteous, holy, pure fellowship with our fellow believers will keep us from unrighteous fellowship and works of darkness. The character of a Christian is those who call on Jesus out of a pure heart. The fruit of the Spirit will emanate from us. These are produced in our lives as we allow God in our lives. This power bestowed upon us by His Spirit will destroy the power of sin, especially the "youthful lusts" and enable us to walk in fellowship with God and our fellow believers (Rom. 8:5-14; 2 Cor. 6:6; Eph. 4:23; Col. 3:12-15; 2Pet. 1:4-9).

"But foolish and unlearned questions avoid, knowing that they do gender strifes."
2:23

Once again Paul cautions against contentions and tells Timothy how to avoid this. *"But foolish and unlearned questions avoid."* There are no benefits in vain and strife of words. Therefore, don't waste your time on these. All that is accomplished from these is that it "genders strife," debates and quarrels among those who call themselves Christians.

"And the servant of the Lord must not strive; but be gentle unto all men, apt to teach, patient,"

"In meekness instructing those that oppo se themselves; if God peradventure will give them repentance to the acknowledging of the truth;"
2: 24-25

" The servant of the Lord must not strive," a servant of God must be gentle to all men, possess a spirit of love, compassion and meekness rather than strife and contention. *"Apt to teach,"* one who strives about cannot teach the Word of God. Men of God must be patient and in love and meekness instruct.

This is the only way a minister can reach a lost and dying world. In the meekness of God exhort the ways of God more perfectly. Our Lord was meek and lowly (Matt. 11:29) therefore, we need to follow his example if we are to reach people with the true gospel, the apostles' doctrine. We can overcome false teachings (evil) with the light (good) true gospel (Rom. 12:21).

"If God, peradventure, will give them repentance to the acknowledging of the truth," repentance is a gift from God. We must correct the (our) opponents

with meekness, and love in hope that God would "haply" grant them repentance (Acts 8:22) and come to know the truth of God's Word. That they would become accurately acquainted with and acknowledge and embrace it.

"And that they may recover themselves out of the snare of the devil, who are taken captive by him at his will."
2:26

The truth shall deliver the sinner out of the snare of the devil. It is only the True Gospel of Jesus Christ that will make one free from sin, destruction, and Satan's dominion. Therefore by ministering the Word of God to the world in meekness, through repentance, they may believe, acknowledge the truth and be delivered from Satan's dominion. When one obeys the Word of God and repents they shall reap joy. For once they were being led captive of the devil and now are led into the glorious liberty found in Jesus. The Lord will deliver us out of all the snares of the enemy if we allow Him to.

"This know also, that in the last days perilous times shall come."
3:1

Understand this, in the last days shortly before Jesus comes back for His church, one without spot, blemish or wrinkle, will come perilous times of great stress, trouble, and tribulation. Things are going to continue to get worse as the end approaches. Wickedness of all sorts is going to increase. The morality of the world will collapse and fail. This time will be a great trying time for God's true servants.

Remember there are wheat and tares, good and evil in the church (Matt. 13:47-k48). Not all who are in the visible kingdom are truly children of God.

Jesus prophesied that seducers would come in with the intent to destroy the church (Matt. 24). Therefore, we must not think it strange when we see this happening.

"For men shall be lovers of their own selves, covetous, boasters, proud, blasphemers, disobedient to parents, unthankful, unholy,"
"Without natural affection, truce-breakers, false accusers, incontinent, fierce, despisers of those that are good,"
"Traitors, heady, highminded, lovers of pleasures more than lovers of God;"
"Having a form of godliness, but denying the power thereof: from such turn away."
3: 2-5

"Lovers of their own selves ," some teach that a lack of love for oneself is the root of sin. However, Paul gives us a list of sins that are all rooted in self-love, a selfish, self-exalting love.

Covetous (philarguros 5366) "moneyloving"
Boasters (alazon 213) "pride, braggart (vagrancy)
Proud (huperephanos 5244) "showing oneself above others, preeminent" "arrogant, disdainful"
Blasphemers (blasphemos 989) "abusive, speaking evil," "railers"
Disobedient (apeithes 545) "unwilling to be persuaded, spurning belief
Unthankful (acharistos 884) ungrateful, thankless
Unholy (anosios 462) "profane"
Without natural affection (astorgos 794) (a, negative, and storge) "love of kindred," especially of parents for children and visa versa.
Trucebreakers (aspondos 786) denotes "without a libation," implacable False accusers (diabolos 1228) "slanderers"
Incontinent (akrates 193) "powerless, impotent," in a moral sense, "unrestrained, without self control"
Fierce (anemeros 434) "not tame, savage"
Despisers (atimos 820) "not loving the good"
Traitors (prodotes 4273) "a betrayer"
Heady (propetes 4312) "precipitate, rash, headstrong Highminded (teuphoo 5187)"conceit," "pride" lifted up with pride, "puffed up"
Pleasures (philedonos 5369) "loving pleasure" of the gratification of the natural desire or sinful desires
Godliness (2150) "to be devout" by a God ward attitude, these had a form of this.

"Without Natural Affection," In these last days there will be a deluge of ungodliness. Satan will set out to destroy the family. They will not have any natural tenderness or love for one another, (i.e. mothers reject or kill their children, Fathers abandon their family, and children neglect their aging parents) men and women will become more lovers of money and worldly pleasures than the things of God.

"Having a Form of Godliness," not everyone who carries a bible or says "Lord, Lord" are true believers. Paul refers to these "religious" people, who profess to be Christian, yet they deny the power which saves them. These people have a façade on and tolerate a sinful lifestyle. Jesus emphatically states that there will be "many" within our churches that will minister in His name and believe they know Him. Yet, they really never knew Him (Matt. 7: 22-23). Remember, Satan himself is transformed into an angel of light. Therefore, it's no great thing that his ministers are transformed as ministers of God (2Cor. 11: 14-15; Matt. 24:24). Yes, they may be called Christians, baptized in Jesus' name and make a show of religion yet they are not of God. From such we are exhorted as true men of God to withdraw ourselves from these false teachers.

"For of this sort are they which creep into houses, and lead captive silly women laden with sins, led away with dives lusts,"
"Ever learning, and never able to come to the knowledge of the truth."
"Now as Jan'nes and Jam'bres withstood Mo'ses, so do these also resist the truth: men of corrupt minds, reprobate concerning the faith."
"But they shall proceed no further: for their folly shall be manifest unto all men, as theirs also was."
3: 6-9

Paul continues to warn Timothy how these seducers will draw away our members unto themselves. They will creep into the houses of believers, portraying to be the same as they are full of love and compassion and draw the people to their house. These proselytes were sully women (weak) and (wicked) laden with sin, and led away with diverse lusts. Someone who is not rooted and grounded in the truth, are easy prey for these seducers. They were close to the truth, *"forever learning"* yet they never advanced in knowledge.

Paul compared these seducers to the magicians who withstood Moses. They *"resisted the truth"* and like them those of our day have corrupt minds, their understandings perverted and *"reprobate concerning their faith."*

Yet, *" they shall proceed no further,"* or much further they attack the weak in our churches, silly and wicked women. Their characters are all the same, *"men of corrupt minds."* Their conduct the same: They *"resist the truth"* they can only go as far as God will permit. Then *"their folly shall be manifest,"* it shall appear that they are imposters and all will see what they are. Every man shall abandon them.

"But thou hast fully known my doctrine, manner of life, purpose, faith, longsuffering, charity, patience,"

"Persecutions, afflictions, which came unto me at An'ti -och, at Ico'ni- um, at Lys'tra; what persecutions I endured: but out of them all the Lord

delivered me."

"Yea, and all that will live godly in Christ Je'sus shall suffer persecution."
"But evil men and seducers shall wax worse and worse, deceiving, and being
deceived."
3: 10-13

" But thou (Timothy) *hast fully known my doctrine."* The more we know the
doctrine of Jesus Christ, the closer we can draw to Him and His Word. Paul's
life was full of trials and tribulation because of the gospel. However, God
never left him and He delivered Paul out of all his troubles. The Psalmist
wrote: *"Many are the afflictions of the righteous: but the Lord delivereth him
out of them all,"* (Ps. 34:19). Paul's purpose was to proclaim the full council
of God (Acts 20:27), to bring many into the knowledge of Jesus Christ. Paul
gave proof of his faith in Jesus Christ. He was longsuffering and patient to
the churches to which he ministered to showing all love and patience toward
all men.

Timothy knew Paul had suffered greatly for the cause of the gospel. " All
who live godly in Christ Jesus shall suffer persecutions," (v.12). Those who
bear the name of Jesus, who clings tenaciously to the Apostles' Doctrine and
who live an exemplary life accordingly will suffer. But we should never fear
because God will deliver us out of them all.

Paul warns Timothy of the fatal end of the seducers. And why it is necessary
not only for Timothy but for us to stay close to the truth, (v.13). As true men
of God we grow better and better. As men of darkness they grow worse and
worse. They deceive and are being deceived. Those who deceive others just
deceive themselves more in the process.

*"But continue thou in the things which thou hast learned and hast been
assured of, knowing of whom thou hast learned them;"*

*"And that from a child thou hast known the holy scriptures, which are able to
make thee wise unto salvation through faith which is in Christ Je'sus."*
3: 14-15

Paul exhorts Timothy to continue in the doctrine that was taught to him by
Paul. It is not enough to learn the doctrines of Jesus Christ, we must continue
in them as well. If we cling tenaciously to the Apostles' Doctrine we will not
be tossed to and fro and carried by every wind of doctrine (Eph. 4:14; Heb.
13:9). Timothy knew the Holy Scriptures from a child. These Holy Scriptures

come from the Holy God. If we are to know, understand, be fully acquainted with the Word and God we must search these Holy Scriptures daily, as the Bereans had," (Acts 17:11).

"All scripture is given by inspiration of God, and is profitable for doctrine, for reproof, for correction, for instruction in righteousness:"
"That the man of God may be perfect, thoroughly fu rnished unto all good works."
3: 16-17

Paul affirms that all scripture is inspired by God. The word inspired (theopneustos 2315) "inspired by God" (theos, "God," pneo, "to breathe"), Thus, "inspired" means, "God-breathed." All scripture is therefore God-breathed; it is the very life and Word of God.

God's Holy inspired Word is infallible; it depicts and is a true witness to His saving activity for mankind through Jesus Christ. No one or anything is equal to its authority. All doctrine and commentaries (even this one) and interpretations must be judged by the Word of God (Deut. 13:3). This Word, His Holy Scriptures must be used in the church as the final authority in all matters for teaching, reproof, correction, doctrine, and instruction in righteous living.

It is the true Word of God and only His inspired Word that will conquer the power of sin our lives (Matt. 4:4; Eph. 6:12, 17; Jas.1:21). If we follow the Word of God, we shall be made men of God, *"perfect and thoroughly furnished to every good work."*

I charge thee therefore before God, and the Lord Je'sus Christ, who shall judge the quick and the dead at his appearing and his kingdom;"
"Preach the word; be instant in season, out of season; reprove, rebuke, exhort with all longsuffering and doctrine."
4: 1-2
"I charge" (diamarturomai 1263) "to testify through and through, bear a solemn witness; hence, "to charge earnestly"

Paul "charged" Timothy in the presence of God and of Christ Jesus to proclaim the gospel as he was called to do. Knowing that he would stand before Jesus in the Day of Judgment and give an answer to everything he had done while on this earth.

When Jesus comes back to claim His church, He shall judge the quick (those found alive) and the dead (those who shall be raised to life out of the grave). When Jesus appears His second time it will be a glorious appearance. He will come and usher in His Kingdom, sitting n the Throne of God, to judge the world.

What was Timothy's charge? He was commissioned as all the disciples were (Matt. 28:19) to preach the Word of God where and whenever an opportunity would arise, whether or not the conditions were favorable, convenient or inconvenient, welcome or unwelcomed. You (and us) are a preacher of the Word of God. Therefore reprove, rebuke and exhort. Call upon the people, to acknowledge their sin, repent, believe on Jesus, be baptized in His name, be filled with His Spirit, and live a holy, pure life before God and men.

We must try to reach a lost dying world in season, when they (the people) want to hear the Word and out of season, even when they do not wish to hear; for it is the Spirit of God that will do the work upon their hearts. We, as men and women of God must not let an opportunity pass by nor neglect our duty under a pretence it is out of season.

We are exhorted to tell the people their faults. Of course this must be done in the love of God and not with a condescending spirit "Reprove". We are to convince them of their wickedness and what the outcome will be if they choose not to heed the warning call (Ez.33:3-6).

We are to exhort, admonish them in the Lord. Encourage them to be faithful, and endure to the end. This is to be done with "all longsuffering and doctrine," teach them the truth as found in Jesus, the Apostles' Doctrine. It is our duty as ministers of the gospel to reclaim them form the darkness and bring them into His marvelous light. So this with diligence, sparing no pain or labour, for our Lord's return is soon and imminent. Why?

"For the time will come when t hey will not endure sound doctrine; but after their own lusts shall they heap to themselves teachers, having itching ears;"

"And they shall turn away their ears from the truth, and shall be turned unto fables."
4: 3-4

"For a time will come when they will not endure sound doctrine." From the very beginning people have always refused sound instructions. The church age is no different, there has always been some who refuse to love sound doctrine; and as our time on the earth comes to a close it is going to only get

worse (3: 1-5; 1Tim. 4:1). Many will profess to be Christians, appear to be good, *"have a form of godliness,"* however they will not tolerate the original New Testament Apostolic Faith which is the "sound doctrine," the apostles' doctrine. They will turn away from the truth and follow after falsehood. They want an easy message.

" After their own lusts shall they heap to themselves teachers," (v. 13). They do not want pastors who preach God's holy standards, they want a pastor who will tell them they can do whatever they want and still be saved. They will not accept God's message of repentance, sin, damnation and the necessity of departing from the world and a walk of holiness.

"The Truth" God's holy inspire d Word must be our ultimate guide. We are to believe, embrace and live according to His Word. We also, must judge or test all teaching churches and organizations by His Word. Many today are turning to and following after manmade doctrines. But, God's true churches will continue in the Apostles Doctrine as taught by Jesus and His disciples. Because so many desire the fables, God shall send them a strong delusion, because they love not the truth (2Thess. 2: 11-12).

"But watch thou in all things, endure afflictions, do the work of an evangelist, make full proof of thy ministry."
4:5

But regardless of what transpires around you, be "watchful in all things." Endure the trials, tribulations and persecutions. Continue doing the work you were called to do, "do the work of an evangelist." And make "full proof of it." Yes, afflictions will come, but endure them. Nevertheless, do not be discouraged, fulfill your ministry. We must make a stand and leave a mark. Refuse to let a natural circumstance (or people) dictate how we serve God (fulfill our ministry).

"For I am now ready to be offered, and the time of my departure is at hand."
"I have fought a good fight, I have finished my course, I have kept the faith:"
4: 6-7

Paul passing the torch to Timothy, he was done; he had completed his work wherein he was called. Now, he encouraged Timothy to do the same. It was with pleasure that Paul looked upon death. For he knew to be absent in the body was to be present with the Lord.

He had "fought a good fight." Paul knew d eath was imminent, and considered his life as a Christian, a minister of the gospel a "good fight," Paul fought against similar things that we fight against: Satan (Eph. 6:12) Jewish or pagan teachings (Rom. 1: 21-22; Gal. 5: 19-21). Judaism- false teachings (Acts 14:19; 4:3-5; 20:28-31; 20:19; Gal. 5:1-6). Immorality in the church (3:5; 4:3; Rom. Ch. 6; 1Cor. 5:1; 6: 9-10) Sin (Rom. 8:13; 1Cor. 9: 24-27) and worldliness (Rom. 12:2).

He never relented on his calling, he finished his course in t he midst of all his trials, he remained faithful to God (Heb. 10:23; 11; 12:1-2). Although he found himself forsaken by fellow believers and opposed by the majority (false teachers) he never compromised the true gospel message, originally given to him by Jesus (1: 13-14; 2:2; 3: 1-16; 1Tim. 6:12).

"Henceforth there is laid up for me a crown of righteousness, which the Lord, the righteous judge, shall give me at that day: and not to me only, but unto all them also that love his appearing."

4:8

Because of Paul's dedication and his faithfulness he had the assurances that he would receive his "crown of righteousness," the crown of life. There is a crown of righteousness available to all who are faithful to Jesus. And at His second coming they all shall receive theirs. God has reserved heavenly rewards for all those who keep the faith in righteousness (Matt. 19:27-29; 2Cor. 5:10).

As Christians we should long for our Lords return. This world is not our home anymore. And we should not feel at home in it. Oh to be united with our Lord and Savior, what a glorious day that shall be. We will be removed from all stress, trials and persecutions. We must be ever watchful and hopeful for our Lord's return.

"Do thy diligence to come shortly unto me:"

"For De'mas hath forsaken me, having loved this present world, and is departed unto Thes-sa-loni'ca; Cres'cens to Ga-la'tia, Titus unto Dal- ma'ti-a."

"Only Luke is with me. Take Mark, and bring him with thee: for he is profitable to me for the ministry."
"And Thych'i-cus have I sent to Eph'e-sus."
"The cloke that I left at Tro'as with Car'pus, when thou comest, bring with thee, and the books, but especially the parchments."

4: 9-15

Paul asks Timothy to come to him quickly if possible. Being an evangelist he was not fixed in any certain church. Therefore he had the liberty to travel to Paul. Paul wanted and desired Timothy to come to him to help him, because several had deserted him.

Demas had left Paul and went back to the world. Demas' first love to Jesus and His gospel was forsaken and he fell in love with the world once again. The love of the world is often associated with apostasy. Crescens had gone one way (Galatia) and Titus another (Dalmatia) (v.10).

Luke (the great physician) was the only one who remained with Paul. He desired the company of his brothers in his final days. That's why his request for Timothy to bring Mark also to help in the ministry. Although Paul and Mark had differences in the past, all was forgiven, they were reconciled. This teaches us as well to have a forgiving spirit. Paul sent Tychicus to the church at Ephesus (v.12).

He had asked Timothy to come to him by the way of Troas. Apparently Paul had left some personal items with Carpus another brother (his cloak). He also asked Timothy to bring his books and especially the parchments. These were probably Paul's original writings of his epistles.

Paul also mentions Alexander and his mischief done to him (v. 14). Alexander was a professed Christian yet he did much evil against Paul. Of course Paul doesn't elaborate on what Alexander had done. Nevertheless, Paul was always in danger not only by his enemies but false brethren as well (1Cor. 11:26). Paul wasn't worried or fearful of these individuals for he knew God would deal with them accordingly.

He warned Timothy to take heed of Alexander, that he would not be betrayed by him as well. As Paul we always have a variety of brothers around us. Some will leave and forsake us and do evil against us, while others will embrace and support us. We should always be watchful for the Demas' and Alexander's in our circle.

"Notwithstanding the Lord stood with me, and strengthened me; that by me the preaching might be fully known, and that all the Gen'tiles might hear: and I was delivered out of the mouth of the lion."

"And the Lord shall deliver me from every evil work, and will preserve me unto his heavenly kingdom: to whom be glory for ever and ever. Amen."
"Salute Pris'ca and A'qui-la, and the household of On-esiph'o-rus."
"E-ras'tus abode at Cor'inth: but Troph'i-mus have I left at Mile'tum sick."
"Do thy diligence to come before winter. Eu-bu'lus greeteth thee, and Pu'dens, and Li'nus, and Clau'di-a, and all the brethren."
"The Lord Je'sus Christ be with thy spirit. Grace be with you. Amen."
4: 16-22

Paul begins to elaborate with Timothy on his present condition. All had forsaken him. Many do not want to suffer as Paul had nor do they want to be associated with Paul because of fear of imprisonment. However Paul prayed to God on their behalf. *"Lord lay it not to their charge."*

Because of the severe persecution against the Christians at Rome no one wanted to be identified with Paul. However Paul says, "The Lord stood with me." To give him the strength he needed to continue to proclaim the gospel to the Gentiles and endure his harsh conditions. If it had not been for Paul's confinement the Gentiles of Rome would not have heard the true gospel. God delivered him "out of the mouth of the lion." This speaks of Nero. He had great confidence in God delivering him from every evil work and for this he gives glory to God. If the Lord be for us, who shall be against us? He it is who strengthens, encourages and preserves us.

Paul continues with salutations to Aquila, and Priscilla, and the household of Onesiphorus (v.19). He mentions leaving Trophimus sick at Miletum (v.20).

He longed for Timothy to come before winter lest he should have a dangerous journey (v21). He sends commendations to him from Eubulus, Pudens, Linus, Claudia and all the brethren.

He closes his epistle with a prayer, " *The Lord Jesus Christ be with thy spirit.*" This alone should bring elation to our hearts, knowing that Jesus is with us and His grace (2Thess. 3: 17-18). It is his grace that teaches us to live holy; His Spirit enables us to do so. His grace is what will preserve us to the end and it is His glory that will crown us hereafter.

For more than 30 years Paul had preached the Word of God faithfully. In appearance, he had gained nothing but pain, suffering and hatred from his own countrymen. Now in prison he awaits death. Yet these do not point to any failure, just the opposite. Paul showed no regrets as he lays his life down for Jesus.

Paul's writings, written from prison are crucial to us as Christians. He led multitudes of people to the true gospel of Jesus Christ. Even today through his epistles he is still winning souls.

Introduction to Titus

This is another one of Paul's Pastoral Epistles. It was written after his release from the first Roman imprisonment, probably between 63 and 65 A.D.

It was written to Titus, one of Paul's converts shortly thereafter Paul left him in charge of the believers in Crete.

Titus was a Gentile (Gal. 2:3) he became a close companion of Paul in the apostolic ministry. Their close friendship is indicated by Paul's reference to him, thirteen times in Paul's other epistles. Titus was a faithful, trustworthy co-worker like Timothy a son (spirited) in the ministry (1:4).

Paul had written this letter to him instructing him to complete his work on the island of Crete. He also conveys his plan to send Artemas or Tychicus to replace him. At which time he could join Paul at Nicopolis (Greece). We know this did occur, for Paul later reassigned him to Dalmatia (2Tim. 4:10).

The primary purpose for this epistle was to set in order the churches of Crete, appointing elders in the church, helping the church to grow in faith and the knowledge of the truth and to silence false teachers.

Paul instructs Titus on the requirements of elders in the church. To teach sound doctrine and rebuke false teachers. Finally Paul emphasizes that good works and a righteous life are the necessary fruits of genuine faith (1:16; 2:7; 3:1, 8, 14; Jas. 2: 14-26).

"Paul, a servant of God, and an apostle of Je'sus Christ, according to the faith of God's elect, and the acknowledging of the truth which is after godliness;"

1:1

Paul was a servant of God, not in the general sense, as a man and a Christian, but especially as a minister serving God in the gospel. Paul was called and appointed by Jesus. His conversion took place on the road to Damascus (Acts 9:3-19). He is described as an apostle of Jesus Christ, one who had seen Him and was commissioned by Him and His doctrine from Him.

" *Truth which is after godliness,*" All gospel truth is after godliness, teaching and nourishing reverence and fear of God and obedience to Him. This truth is not only to be known but acknowledged as well. Paul's commission was to promote the faith of God's chosen ones and lead them to discernment and recognition of an acquaintance with the truth which will lead to godliness.

No church can claim to teach the sound doctrine of the apostle's if it doesn't lead their congregation to a life of godliness. The true gospel will produce godliness.

"In hope of eternal life, which God, that cannot lie, promised before the world began;"
2:2

The only limitation God has is that what He has placed upon Himself or those resulting from His moral nature. Since He is holy and sinless, He abides by His own moral character. Therefore, it is impossible for God to lie or contradict His own Word. The truthfulness of God applies to His Word in all scripture. Because scripture in the inspired Word of God, it is completely true and trustworthy.

The faith and godliness of believers leads to eternal life and gives hope and an expectation of eternal life.
"But hath in due times manifested his word through preaching, which is committed unto me according to the commandment of God our Saviour:"
1:3

God has ma nifested His word through the preaching of men. *"Faith comes by hearing and hearing by the word of God,"* by the Word preached, which was committed unto Paul. Paul was called and appointed to preach the word of God. "Woe is unto me if I preach not the gospel," (1Cor. 9:16).

Notice: " *God our Saviour.*" We have only one God and one Saviour. They are one in the same. All the fulness of the Godhead resides in Jesus bodily (Col. 2:9). Only God was sinless, but He did not have flesh and blood. Therefore He prepared Himself a body (Heb. 10:5) that He might shed His innocent blood to save humanity. There is one God and Jesus is God, our Saviour. There is only one Spirit of God, and since the Holy Spirit is the

Spirit of Christ we receive Christ into our lives when we are filled or baptized with the Holy Spirit (Rom. 8:9). Jesus is the I Am (Jn. 8:24; Ex.3: 14-15).

"To Ti'tus, mine own son after the common faith: Grace, mercy, and peace, from God the Father and the Lord Je'sus Christ our Saviour."
1:4

To Titus, mi ne own son (Paul's spiritual son) for he begot Titus by the supernatural regeneration (1Cor. 4:15). The common faith is that which all the apostle's and disciples of Jesus taught. Jude exhorts us to contend "fight for" this common faith (v.3).

As in verse 3 we should consider the dual nature of Jesus in this scripture. The term "Father" refers to God Himself – God in all His deity. When we speak of the eternal Spirit of God, we mean God Himself, the Father. "God the Father," is a perfectly acceptable and biblical phrase.

The general context of the salutations themselves shows that the writers emphasized two different manifestations of God, and all these New Testament greetings focus on the two roles of God as Father and Son.

"…Grace, mercy and peace fr om
God the Father even [Kai] our Lord
Jesus Christ our Saviour:"

All grace, mercy and peace come from above, from God the Father (Spirit). God is a spirit (Jn. 4:24), and from our Lord Jesus Christ. He, God the Father of all by creation, but of the good by adoption through Jesus our Saviour and through regeneration by His Spirit, all is by Jesus, who is Lord of all, our redeemer and Head.

"For this cause left I thee in Crete, that thou shouldest set in order the things that are wanting, and ordain elders in every city, as I had appointed thee:"
1:5

This is the job of an evangelist (Titus was in the office of) to set in order the things that are undone in the church and to appoint elders. Setting things in order was of a spiritual application such as: Spiritual ordinances, and appointments which derived from Jesus. This setting was left up to Titus.

Titus was to ordain elders in every city. Those who followed and obeyed the apostle's doctrine, these elders were to have the care and charge of the local church, to feed and govern them, those who labored in Word and doctrine.

"If any be blameless, the husband of one wife, having faithful children not accused of riot or unruly."
1:6

Paul gives Titus directions about ordination, showing whom he should ordain and whom not. If any be blameless (anenkletos 410) "nothing laid to ones charge" (as the result of public investigation). Blameless implies not merely acquittal, but the absence of even a charge or accusation against a person. This is to be the case with elders.

A Christian leader (Elder, Bishop, Deacon Etc.) must be an example of the believers (1Tim. 4:12; 1Pet. 5:3). That is to say live a life of holiness, one which someone would find worthy to imitate.

A Bishop (overseer) must be an example to the family of God, especially his faithfulness to his wife and children. If he cannot take care of his house, how can he take care of the house of God (1Tim. 3:5)? He must be the "husband of one wife" (1Tim. 3:2). An overseer therefore should be a believer who has remained faithful to his wife. The literal translation of the Greek (mias hunaikos, an attribute genitive) is "a one-woman man," i.e. the faithful husband of his wife.

Any persons within the church who are guilty of serious sin must disqualify themselves from the office of a pastor or any leadership disqualify themselves from the office of a pastor or any leadership 12). God has made it clear, *"they must be blameless."* This doesn't mean God will not forgive, for God certainly will forgive any sin listed in 1Tim. 3: 1-3. One cannot be living in sin and be in a leadership position.

"For a bishop must be blameless, as the steward of God; not selfwilled, not soon angry, not given to wine, no striker, not given to filthy lucre;"
1:7

The terms "Elder" (presbuteris v.5) and "Bishop" (episkopos v.7) are synonymous and refer to the same church office. Elder points to a spiritual maturity and dignity required for the office; a bishop refers to an overseer of the church.

God insist that His bishops have a high moral godly standard. If the leaders of God's church are not blameless, neither will the church be. There will be no guidance no examples for them to follow. As a steward of God a bishop must not be:

Selfwilled (authades 829) "self-pleasing" (autos, "self," hedomai, "to please), denotes one who is dominated by self-interest, and inconsiderate for others, arrogantly asserts his own will.

Not soon angry (mi orgilon) not one of a hasty temper; soon and easily provoked. A bishop must be gentle, meek and patient to all men.

Not given to wine: he must be sober not a drunkard. Abstinence from intoxicating wine or other beverages is a requirement for the elders of God's church. They are to be a holy vessel before God and men, an example. One cannot be filled with wine and the Spirit of God at the same time (Eph. 5:18).

No striker (plektes 4131) "a brawler." In any quarrelsome or contentious manner. Not to be cruel or show unnecessary roughness.
Not given to filthy lucre (aischrokerdes 146) denotes "greedy of base gains"

But a bishop is to be a lover of hospitality. He is to use what he has to help others. Receiving and entertaining strangers is good and pleasing to God.

Bishops must be a lover of good men, or of good things. This will be evidenced by their piety, and likeness to our Lord and Savior Jesus Christ. *"Do good to all men, especially the household of faith,"* (Gal.6:10).

Sober (sophron 4998) denotes "of sound mind" (sozo, "to save," phren, "the mind"); hence, "self-controlled, sober minded," a minister must be a wise steward, not rash, foolish or heady.

Just (dikaios 13420)"righteous," a state of being right, or right conduct, moral righteousness
Holy (hosios 3741) signifies "religiously right, holy." One who worships and reverences God
Temperate (enkrates 1468) denotes "exercising self-control"

Sober in respect of himself, just and righteous towards all men and holy towards God. Now, this is what a bishop should be and what he should not be.

"But a lover of hospitality, a lover of good men, sober, just, holy, temperate;"
"Holding fast the faithful word as he hath been taught, that he may be able by sound doctrine both to exhort and to convince the gainsayers."
1: 8-9

The duty of a Bishop (elder) is to" *hold fast the faithful Word, as he has been taught.*" Keeping and teaching the doctrine of Jesus and His apostles. As Paul declared, "I have not shunned to *declare unto you all the counsel of God,*" (Acts 20:27). Ministers today need to be able to say the same, and will by clinging tenaciously to the true doctrine.

We are to hold to the doctrine in order that we might be able to exhort, draw others to the truth in Jesus Christ and to convince the gainsayers, those of the contrary mind. It was Titus duty to exhort and minister to those who wanted to hear the gospel, and convince those who contradict the apostles' teaching. This can only be accomplished by holding fast to the sound doctrine.

"For there are many unruly ad vain talkers and deceivers, specially they of the circumcision:"
1:10

The unruly (anupotaktos 506) "not subject to rule" (a, negative, n, euphonic, hupotasso, "to put in subjection) "disobedient" persons. "Not subject." These individuals were headstrong and had ambitions of power. They refuse to submit to any authority except their own.

Vain talkers (mataiologos 3151) "talking idly" (mataios, "vain, idle," lego, "to speak")

Deceivers (phrenapates 5423) "leading astray, seducing" or "a mind - deceiver" These vain talkers and deceivers are of those of the circumcision party who have come over from Judaism.

"Whose mouths must be stopped, who subvert whole houses, teaching things which they ought not, for filthy lucre's sake." 1:11

These trouble makers must be stopped. Titus was to show them their error according to the Holy Scriptures. Faithful ministers must oppose seducers in good time that their folly be made manifest (open before all) that it should precede no further (2Tim, 3:9). The reason for this is because they (the false teachers) were subverting whole houses (families) they were teaching things that they should not have been teaching, for the purpose of getting (namely the law of Moses, circumcision) base advantage and disreputable gain.

"One of themselves, even a prophet of their own, said, The Cre'ti-ans are always liars, evil beasts, slow bellies."
"This witness is true. Wherefore rebuke them sharply, that they may be sound in the faith;"
"Not giving heed to Jew'ish fables, and commandments of men, that turn

from the truth.”
1: 12-14

“ One of themselves, even a prophet of their own,” That is to say a Cretan not a Jew. Here was their testimony. “The Cretians are always liars, evil beast, and slow bellies.” They were compared and accused of falsehood, evil beast for their savage nature and slow bellies for their laziness.

Paul brings the affirmation of the accusations stating *“ This witness is true.”* Paul himself verified that the testimony against the Cretians was true, and he instructs Titus how to deal with them, *“Rebuke them sharply.”* Paul in a letter to Timothy instructed him to rebuke with meekness, but to Titus, *“Rebuke them sharply.”* The Cretians corruptions were many and gross, committed without shame or modesty. Obviously some sin was dealt with in different manners than other. *“Of some have compassion, making a difference; and others save with fear, pulling them out of the fire,”* (Jude 23-24).

The reason for such a sharp rebuke, “That they may be sound in the faith.” Not to give heed to Jewish myths or fables or to manmade rules and regulations who reject the truth. Te sharp rebuke is not to be done with malicious intent, but with love and compassion to reclaim and reform the erroneous and the guilty. Titus was to bring them (the Cretians) back to the sure foundation, to the apostles’ doctrine, the sound faith, and that they not continue or give heed to Jewish fables and commands of men.

“Unto the pure all things are pure: but unto them that are defiled and unbelieving is nothing pure; but even their mind and conscience is defiled.”
1:15

Paul is referring to meats and drinks and such as was forbidden under the law, (some still maintained these observances and tried to teach others to do so). *“But unto them that are defiled and unbelieving is nothing pure.”* Things which are good they abuse and turn to sin. They are corrupt in all they do. Their very minds and consciences are defiled and polluted. *“The sacrifice of the wicked is an abomination to the Lord,”* (Prov. 15:8).

Paul emphasizes that if a person’s moral condition is pure, and then distinction between unclean and clean meats has no moral meaning to him. *“They profess that they know God; but in works they deny him, being abominable, and disobedient, and unto every good work reprobate,”*
1:16

They profess to know God (recognize perceive and be acquainted with Him). There are many today who in word profess to know God, yet their lifestyles and conversations deny Him. In other words their practice is in contradiction to their profession. Oh, they looked good and talked good but they were fullof dead men's bones, (Ez. 33:31; Matt. 23:27-28). These leaders appeared righteous, but their hearts were full of hypocrisy, pride, lust and sin. Yes, they were beautiful and attractive on the outside, they looked like Christians. Yet on the inside they were vile and corrupt.

"But speak thou the things which become sound doctrine:"
2:1

But you (Titus) speak those things which become sound doctrine, regardless what others speak. Speak what is agreeable to God's Word, things that are pure and uncorrupt. The apostles' doctrines are the sound doctrines. As elders (ministers) we must be careful to preach only biblical truths. Now Paul instructs Titus to apply this sound doctrine to several types of persons in the church.

"That the aged men be sober, grave, temperate, sound in faith, in charity, in patience."
2:2

Older men must be an example to all believers. They must present, (as well as all Christians) themselves as a living sacrifice to God without the use of wine (intoxicating drinks) (1Tim. 3:2, 11; Rom. 12:1-2).

Sober (nephalios 3524) "circumspect" The Greek lexiuns have the primary meaning as "abstaining from wine."

"The word originally denotes abstinence from alcohol" (Reinecher and Rogers) "one who does not drink wine" (Greek dictionary of Byzantius, Athens, 1839); "Not with wine, wine less" (Liddell and Scott); "free from all infusion of wine" (Moulton-Mulligan); "holding no wine' (G. Abbott-Smith); "literally, of a state of abstinence from wine" (Brown, dictionary of New Testament Theology, Vol. 1) Brown adds, "Nephalios occurs only in the pastoral epistles and denotes the abstinence style of life required of bishop (1Tim. 3:2). Women (1Tim, 3:11), and elders (Titus 2:2)." R. Laird Hanis states that "it is used regularly in the classical authors meaning free from all wines" (The Bible Today, pg. 139).

Jewish writers, contemporaries of Paul and Peter, confirmed the common use of the primary definition. Josephus states in reference to Jewish priests that "they are in all respects pure and abstinent (nephalioli), being forbidden to drink wine while they wear the priestly robe" (antiquities, 3. 12.2) Philo states that the regenerate soul "abstains (nephein) continually and during the whole of its life" (drunkenness, 37).

Therefore, in light of all these references, it cannot be reasonably supposed that Paul used this term without knowledge of its dominant meaning (1Thess. 5:6).

Grave (semnos 4586) first denoted "reverend, august, venerable" then "serious, grave," whether of persons
Temperate (nephalios 3524) "sober" "vigilant" (sober minded)
Sound Faith (pistis 4102) "a sincere and steadfast, constantly adhering to the truth of the gospel.
In charity (agape 26) "affection or benevolence"

Christian love, whether exercised toward the brethren or toward men generally, is not an impulse from the feelings, it does not always run with the natural inclinations nor does it spend itself only upon those for whom some affinity is discovered. Love seeks the welfare of all, (Rom. 15:2) and works no ill to any, (Rom. 13:8-10). Love seeks opportunity to do good to all men, and especially toward them that are of the household of faith. (Gal. 6:10; 1Cor. 13; Col. 3:12-14).

In patience (hupomone 5281) "an abiding under" (hupo, "under," meno, "to abide") Persistence, perseverance" a "longsuffering"
"The aged women likewise, that they be in behavior as becometh holiness, not false accusers, not given to much wine, teachers of good things;
2:3

The women must also be instructed and warned. They must be devout in their department, not gossipers or slanderers, but behave as becometh holiness. They must walk and talk as a child of God, giving an example for others to follow. They should keep a pious decency and decorum in clothing and gesture, which is proper for a holy person. *"Whatever you do, do all to the glory of God,"* (1Cor. 10:31) and whatever things are good, godly, or becometh holiness look upon and do (Phil. 4:8).

False accusers (diablos 1228) (mi diabolous) "no calumniators or sowers of discord"

Women are not to slander and back-bite their neighbors. A slanderer is one *"whose tongue is set on fire of hell"* (Jas. 3:6). Sins of speech include harsh and unkind words, lying, and exaggeration, teaching false doctrine, gossiping, and boasting. Because of one's tendency to sin with our tongues we are to *"be swift to hear, slow to speak, slow to wrath,"* (Jas. 1:19).

They are to be "teachers of good things." They are not only to teach by example of a holiness walk but also by doctrinal instructions at home (Prov. 31:1, 26). Teach the younger women to be sober (wise), to love their husbands, and to love their children.

"That they may teach the young women to be sober, to love their husbands, to love their children,"
"To be discreet, chaste, keepers at home, good, obedient to their own husbands, that the word of God be not blasphemed."
2: 4-5

God has given the women a specific task of caring for the children He has entrusted to them (1Tim. 5:14). To be a helper and faithful companion to her husband (Gen. 2:18), caring in her home for elderly parents (1Tim. 5:8; Jas. 1:27).

To be discreet (sophron 4998) "of sound mind selfcontrolled," "sober-minded," "Temperate"
Chaste (hagnos 53) "pure from every fault, immaculate" "pure from carnality, modest," "PURE" Holy as being free from defilement

Woman should give no advantage to the enemy, to allow them to speak reproachfully. They are to guide the house. Where there is true love she will have no problem loving and being obedient to her husband (1Tim. 2L12) Why? (1Tim. 2: 13-14; Eph. 5:22-23).

Jesus is the head of the church, to protect and save it, and so the husband is over the wife, to keep her from injuries, and provide for her. Therefore, as the church is subject to Jesus, so let the *"wives be unto their own husbands, as is fit in the Lord"* (Col. 3:18). In doing so, *"the word of God be not blasphemed."*

"Young men likewise exhort to be sober minded."
"In all things shewing thyself a pattern of good works: in doctrine shewing uncorruptness, gravity, sincerity,"
2: 6-7

Young men are likewise exhorted to be sober minded (discreet), considerate, not rash, advisable and submissive (humble).

Clearly with Paul's instructions to Titus he would be able to teach the aged men and women, the younger men and women the ways of the Lord. Titus could not very well teach these principles to others unless he himself led by example conducted himself appropriately.

" *In all things showing thyself a pattern of good works.*" If Titus had not done this his message would be obscured and confusing. He would be tearing down what he was trying to build. One needs to practice what they preach. Lead by example. When they see purity, gravity, sobriety and all good life, in thee (Titus) and us as leaders, they may be more easily won to a life of holiness in Christ Jesus. Ministers must be examples to the flock, in all that they do, whether in doctrine or speech must be accordingly as to not bring any condemnation upon the ministers (1Tim. 4:12). Thus we need to be an example in word, in conversation, the live corresponding with the doctrine of Jesus Christ. In doing so we "*shalt both save thyself* (ourselves) *and those that hear thee,*" (us) (1Tim. 4:16).

"Sound speech, that cannot be condemned; that he that is of the contrary part may be ashamed,having no evil thing to say of you."
2:8

The reason there is such a strict code of righteous conduct for the elders and that his message be sound is *"that he who is of the contrary part may be ashamed, having no evil thing to say of you."*

Christians in general, not just elders are under a microscope per say. People are always watching them. They look for us to make a mistake, to stumble or fall. However, if we, "In all things show ourselves a pattern of good works" they cannot find a fault. And when they do speak evil of us as an evildoer, let them be ashamed who falsely accused us. Lets' keep our conversation in Christ (1Pet. 3:16).

"Exhort servants to be obedient unto their own masters, and to please them well in all things; not answering again;"

Servants are still obligated to please God in their conduct as well. Servants are to respect and do their duties to their earthly masters, while keeping their eyes and heart turned to God. Servants are exhorted to be obedient to their masters according to God's will.

Servants are to please their master in all things. Not as men-pleasers, but as unto the Lord. While they serve, they are submissive unto God (Eph. 6: 5-7). They can be a servant of man and yet be a servant to Christ, these are not contrary but sub ornate.

"Not answering again," Do not contradict, dispute, argue, or provoke your masters. Of course masters are to treat their servants well also.
"Not purloining (nosphizo 3557) "to set apart, remove," "to set apart for oneself, to purloin." "Keep"
"But showing all good fidelity (pistis 4102) "faith, faithfulness,"

Not only must a servant help promote his masters prosperity; he must not steal from him. In his faithfulness he is ready to execute his masters' wishes, to dispatch his affairs and the keeping of his secrets. In this way he brings the blessings of God upon himself. *"If you have not been faithful in that which is another man's, who shall give you that which is your own?"* (Luke 16:12).

If they, the servants, obey their masters in all things according to the will of God, *"they may adorn the doctrine of God our Saviour in all things."* That is through their actions as a humble, obedient servant they can recommend the gospel to others.

Salvation in Jesus Christ is for one and all, whether Jew or Gentile, bond or free. All are equal in the eyes of God.
"For the grace of God that bringeth salvation hath appeared to all men."

Let all people, men, women, and children, young and old, bond or free be about the Father's business. Fulfill their Christian duties, for we are all put under the grace of God.

This saving grace instructs us to decisively reject the ungodly passions and pleasures, of this present world and regard them as abominable (Rom. 1:18-32; 2Tim. 2:22; 1Jn. 2: 15-17). It is His grace that gives the believer power to live righteously and godly while waiting for Jesus to return.

This "Grace of God" is not of respect. It has appeared to ALL men. Not just a certain group of people, (i.e. Jews). The gospel is open and available to all and all are invited to partake of the benefits thereof (Rom. 16: 25-26).

"Teaching us that, denying ungodliness and worldly lusts, we should live soberly, righteously, and godly, in this present world;"
2:12
The grace of God has not only been manifest to all, but has come to teach us.

It directs those who partake of it what to shun and what to follow, what to do and what to avoid.

In order for us to walk a life of "holiness and righteousness" we must shun, turn away from the kingdom of Satan (i.e. the world). Every true believer must strive for a life of holiness even in the midst of an evil world. This holy life is possible in Him, "before Him," in His presence (Luke 1:75).

Grace instructs us to deny ungodliness and worldly lusts. We are to renounce and have nothing more to do with the works of the flesh. "Put off, concerning the former conversation, the old man which is corrupt; (Eph. 4:22) all that is in the world is not of the Father, but is of this world (1Jn, 2:16). All the lusts of the world shall pass away, *but he that doeth the will of God abideth forever,*" (1Jn. 2:17).

We are to live:

Soberly (sophronos 4996) "self controlled" it suggests the exercise of that self-restraint that governs all passions and desires, enabling the believer to be conformed to the mind of Christ.

Righteously (dikaios 1346) "Justly" in accordance with what is right.
Godly (eusebos21530 denotes "piously, godly," "to live" (of manner of life)

"In this present world," We are to live in respect of others (soberly), righteously toward all men, godly towards God in our manner of life. We live this life now, on this earth, not when we are taken away from it to be with Jesus. Right Now, today!

The "grace of God" the gospel of Jesus Christ teaches us how to believe and hope, also how to live in this present world. To have faith and hope in something better, to which our living sober, righteous and a godly life is preparative.

"Looking for that blessed hope, and the glorious appearing of the great God and our Saviour Je'sus Christ;"
2:13

"Looking for that blessed hope" is the glorious appearing of our Great God and Savior Jesus Christ. This hope is capable of being realized at any time (Matt. 24:42; Luke 12: 36-40; Jas. 5: 7-9).

We are promised a resurrection with our Lord. We shall live forever in our redeemed bodies with the Lord (1Thess. 4: 13-18). Believers today must be ever watchful and hopeful for our great God's return to take us out of this evil corrupt world and unto Himself (Rom. 13:11; 1Cor. 7:29; 10:11; 5: 51-52; Phil. 4:5).

"Who gave himself for us, that he might redeem us from all iniquity, and purify unto himself a peculiar people, zealous of good works."
2:14 Jesus shed His blood on the cross in order to redeem us from all iniquity.
Redeem (lutroo 3084) "to release on receipt of ransom" signifying "to release by paying a ransom price, to redeem"

Ransom conveys the meaning of a price paid to obtain freedom of others. In the redemptive work of Jesus, His death is the price paid to deliver us from the dominion of Satan, (sin), (1Tim. 2:6; Matt. 20:28).

To purify (katharizo 2511) "to cleanse, make free form admixture," "cleansing"
Cleansing to make us holy people, separated from sin and the world to be God's own special possession.

Jesus died shedding His blood to redeem all of mankind from darkness. Those still struggling with sin need to know that if Jesus died for them, He will also give them power over the enemy (Rom. 5: 9-11). Our salvation lies only in the blood of Jesus and His resurrection life. We have been reconciled to God through Jesus Christ.

Through this act of love we have been redeemed, set free, made a peculiar people. To live in sin is to trample underfoot the redeeming blood, and reject the benefits of it.

God purchased His church with His own blood (Acts 20:28). No mere man could do this, but the Son of God could. He gave Himself for His church, to cleanse it, as a sinless sacrifice. We are purified through and by His precious blood.

We are a chosen generation, a royal priesthood, a holy nation, and so a peculiar people. Zealous of good works, the "grace of God" the doctrine of Jesus Christ, the gospel is not a doctrine of the mundane, but of holiness and good life (1Pet. 2:9).

"These things speak, and exhort, and rebuke with all authority. Let no man despise thee."
2:15

These things mentioned afore hand are not Jewish customs or manteachings, but of God. Speak these things to one and all who will lend you an ear. Exhort and rebuke with all authority. Do not neglect to teach the full council of God (Acts 22:27).

The most effectual way for ministers to secure themselves from contempt is to teach and preach the apostles' doctrine, and to follow the examples of our Lord and Savior Jesus Christ.

"Put them in mind to be subject to principalities and powers, to obey magistrates, to be ready to every good work,"
3:1

Titus was to remind the people to be in subjection (submit) to principalities and powers, to obey magistrates. Believers must be obedient to civil and governmental authorities, obey civil law, and be good citizens as long as these governmental laws do not conflict with God's laws (Acts 5:29).

"To speak evil of no man, to be no brawlers, but gentle, shewing all meekness unto all men."
3:2

To speak evil of no man, whether unjustly and falsely or unnecessarily, without call, when it does harm and not any good to the person. As the old cliché goes, "if you cannot say anything nice, don't say anything at all. Such uncharitable talk is displeasing to God (Prov. 17:9).

Remind the people of this as well as not to be brawlers (fighters) either with gainsaying (by mouth) or a physical altercation. Believers must follow after things which are conducive to peace (Phil. 4:8).

Wherefore, be gentle, meek and mild toward all men. Not only to have a gentle heart but relay the love of God in our words and actions toward others. Why?

"For we ourselves also were sometimes foolish, disobedient, deceived, serving divers lusts and pleasures, living in malice and envy, hateful and hating one another."

3:3

For we at one time were foolish, disobedient, deceived, serving divers lusts and pleasures, living in malice and envy, hateful, and hating one another. Before Jesus this was our nature (fleshly) now in Jesus we have a new nature (spiritual). Therefore, be patient with those who have not yet attained to where you have.

Foolish (anoetus 453) signifies "not understanding" (a, negative, noeo, "to perceive, understand." Also "describes one who does not govern his own lusts.

Disobedient (apeithes 545) "unwilling to be persuaded, spurning belief, disobedient," or" obstinacy, obstinate, rejection of the will of God." Deceived (planao 4102) "to go astray, wander"

We ourselves were foolish without true spiritual understanding and knowledge, ignorant of heavenly things. We were disobedient, heady, resisting the Word and those who spoke it to us. We were deceived or wandered out of the ways of truth and holiness.

Since we were all the above we were easily ensnared by the lusts of our flesh. We became a servant of sin. We were living in malice. Malice desires to hurt another individual and rejoices in this action. We were jealous, envious of another's prosperity, or blessings. Maybe someone had more money, better house or car, or even our brothers who preached, taught or sang better than us. We had such jealousy that we had hatred toward these people.

Those living in sin despise God and the men of God. They are hateful toward them. They actually hate one another. Yes, we were here. However, we have been delivered and set free in the name of Jesus. These things should not be our character now. We are new creatures in Christ Jesus. Old things are passed away, all things become new (2Cor. 5:17). We have a renewed knowledge (Col. 3:10) and understanding (Rom. 12:2) and living a life of holiness (Eph. 4:24). We are a new person (Gal. 6:15); Eph. 2:10, 15; 4:28; Col.3:10).

"But after that the kindness, and love of God our Saviour toward man appeared,"

Not by works of righteousness which we have done, but according to his mercy he saved us, by the washing of regeneration, and renewing of the Ho'ly Ghost;"

3: 4-5

But when the goodness, love and kindness of our Lord and Savior Jesus Christ the true living God (1Jn. 5:20) appeared to us, we by His mercy and grace were changed into vessels of honor (Rom. 9:21).

Jesus saved us according to His mercy. Not because we done works of righteousness nor deserved salvation. It was His act of love upon a backslidden, sinful people. Those saved will produce works of righteousness, not to be saved, but because they are saved.

We are a new creature in Christ Jesus. All our evil habits are done away with. We have new thoughts and desires.

"He saved us." It is an expression already present. However, we must be initially saved now, by regeneration. Without regeneration there is no first resurrection in the Holy Ghost. Without the first resurrection we have no second resurrection.

The washing of regeneration, this work is both outward and an inward spiritual work. First, water is of a cleansing and purifying nature, it washes away the filth of the flesh. In the like manner it signifies doing away with the guilt and defilement of sin by the blood of Jesus. Thus, baptism in water, in the name of Jesus doth also save us (Acts 2:38; Acts 22:16; Eph. 5:26; 1Pet. 3:21).

Baptism in the name of Jesus is an outward sign and seal of salvation. We were commanded by Jesus to be baptized in the name of (Matt. 28:19).

We were born again of water and "the renewing of the Holy Ghost" Spirit, we are quickened (made alive) and sanctified by the Spirit. Through His Spirit we can put off our old man. "If we walk in the Spirit, we will not fulfill the lusts of the flesh (Gal 5:16).

"Which he shed on us abundantly through Je'sus Christ our Saviour:
3:6

God has shed His Spirit upon us in abundance (Isa. 44:3; Joel 2:28). These were prophecies of what God was going to do in the church era. The prophecies were fulfilled in the day of Pentecost (Acts 2:17, 18, 33, 38; 10:44-45). The Holy Ghost fell on all men Gentiles and Jews alike.

Our salvation is only through Jesus Christ. All we have a need of is in Him. He is the Father (by Him all things were made), He is the Son who shed His blood for us) He is the Holy Spirit (Christ in you the hope of glory), Father in creation– Son in redemption-Holy Ghost in regeneration.

God has supplied us with an abundant and adequate supply of His grace and power as a result of our new birth and the Holy Spirit works in us.
"That being justified by his grace, we should be made heirs according to the

hope of eternal life."

"this is a faithful saying, and these things I will that thou affirm constantly, that they which have believed in God might be careful to maintain good works. These things are good and profitable unto men."

3: 7-8 Here is why our salvational experience is so important. That we might be justified,
Justification (dikaioo 1344) "to deem to be right" "To be righteous"

Our justification is by the grace of God. It is through our salvational process that we become heirs and joint-heirs with Christ, of eternal life. Without justification there is no sonship, no right of inheritance (Jn. 1:12). Eternal life is a promise to all who believe, obey and trust in Jesus.

This salvational message is the most trustworthy. Paul exhorted Titus to re-assert strongly this message on a daily basis. So that they which have trusted in relied on and believed in God, may show forth the fruit of righteousness. To conduct and apply themselves honorable and to doing well, for such are excellent and profitable for the people.

It is the responsibility of God's ministers to teach and preach sound doctrine and good in itself. In affirming the salvational message one saves not only themselves, but them that hear you. It's sound doctrine that puts a person in the church of Jesus Christ and keeps one there.

"But avoid foolish questions, and genealogies, and contentions, and strivings about the law; for they are unprofitable and vain."
3:9

Now, after Paul had given instructions to Titus on what to teach, he proceeds to give him instructions on what to avoid. Avoid stupid and foolish controversies and genealogies and dissensions and wrangling about the law.

Those of the Mosaic rites and ceremonies wanted traditions to continue in the church. However, Jesus superseded the man-made ceremonies of ordinaries and done away with them.

Ministers must not only teach sound doctrine but they must also shun and oppose things which are contrary to the doctrine of Jesus Christ and His apostles'. Because there will be heresies and heretics in the church Paul instructs Titus what to do in such a case and how to deal with them.

"A man that is a heretick after the first and second admonition reject;"

3:10

Heretics are false teachers who teach man-made traditions and ideologies which are contrary to the Word of God. By their teachings they create division within the church. After a second admonition proves ineffective, these heretics must be rejected (i.e. expelled from church membership). Those who reject the apostles' doctrine, the true gospel of Jesus Christ, and insert their own ideas are sinning (v.11). He who forsakes the truth and propagates false doctrine, and breaks peace within the church after due means used to reclaim him, must be rejected.

"Knowing that he that is such is subverted, and sinneth, being condemned of himself."
3:11

Knowing that he that is such is subverted (turned off from the foundation) and sinneth grievously, being self-condemned. Those who will not heed to correction, but are obstinate in their errors are subverted and self-condemned. Therefore, even if they are rejected because they would not heed to righteous reprove bring they inflict that punishment on themselves. In other words the elders didn't cast them out of the church, they did it themselves. They are self-condemned. The church must preserve its' pureness and deal with the heretics accordingly. If not the entire church will be subverted-perverted.

"When I shall send Ar'te-mas unto thee, or Tych'i-cus, be diligent to come unto me to Nicop'o-lis: for I have determined there to winter." "Bring Ze'nas the lawyer and Apol'los on their journey diligently, that nothing be wanting unto them."
3: 12-13

Paul had asked Titus to join him at Nicopolis as soon as Artemas or Tychicus could replace him at Crete. Titus apparently was not a church bishop, but an evangelist. Otherwise Paul would not have requested him to leave his church to be with him.

Artemas is not mentioned anywhere else in the Bible. However, Tychicus is mentioned several times. Paul calls him a beloved brother, a faithful minister and a fellow servant in the Lord.

Paul had also requested that Titus would bring two of his friends with him. Zenas, the lawyer, and Apollos, who was an eminent and faithful minister and a Jew born at Alexandria (Acts 20:24).

"And let ours also learn to maintain good works for necessary uses, that they be not unfruitful."
3:14

Once again Paul reiterates what he had instructed Titus previously (v.8), *"Let ours also learn to maintain good works."* Not only elders but all believers who believe in God, learn to maintain good works. "Good works" are the result of the indwelling Spirit in the believers' life (vv 4-8). Believers must be a "pattern of good works" (2:7), "Zealous of good works" (4:14) "ready [for] every good works' (v.8), and they must "learn to maintain good works."

Being a minister (a Christian) is not a fruitless profession. Believers must be filled with the fruits of righteousness, which are by Jesus Christ, to the glory and praise of God. They must not only be profitable but harmless as well. Doing good and eschewing evil.

"All that are with me salute thee. Greet them that love us in the faith. Grace be with you all. Amen."
3:15

Paul concludes his letter to Titus with salutations and benedictions. He tells Titus to "greet those that love us in the faith, or for the faith, who are fellow believers, fellow servants in the Lord.

" Grace be to all." Not just Titus but those who are with him as well. Though this epistle was written to Titus, it was to be read to the church as well. "Grace to all." Paul wished/prayed that the grace of God would be upon all of them. This is a great respect or recognition to others. It is summarily, all good. Amen closes his prayer, so it shall be.

A BRIEF SUMMARY
REPENTANCE

WHY DO WE NEED TO REPENT?

The reason we must repent is that the Bible tells us that all of us have sinned. Sin separates us from God. When we repent, God removes the sin that keeps us from Him.

WHAT IS SIN? Sin is breaking the Law of God. We all live by certain laws or rules; at home, work, school or play. If we disobey or break the law, we will be punished.

EXAMPLE: We have laws that govern how we drive our cars. The law says that we must stop at red lights. If you run a red light, a police officer could stop you and give you a ticket. If you paid the fine you would be forgiven. If you did not pay the fine, you could go to jail.

We all know that it is wrong to lie to your parents. If you tell them you picked up your toys when you did not, that would be breaking the law. Your mother may make you stay in your room for two hours after school as punishment.

So we can see that sin is when we break the law of God. God is the ultimate authority in the uni9verse. He has told us certain things in the Bible that we should not do, such as lying, stealing, or being disrespectful to our parents.

WHAT HAPPENS WHEN WE SIN? When we sin or break the Law of God, it is put on our record like a conduct grade in school. Every sin has a penalty or fine attached to it. Sin is not free; somebody has to pay for it! Paying a penalty is another way of saying punishment.

We also know that God is holy and righteous in every way, and cannot live in our heart if sin is there. Sin separated us from God! Therefore, we must get it out of our heart before Jesus can come and live inside us.

WHAT IS REPENTANCE?

Repentance is admitting to God that we have broken His law and that we are sorry. We are also asking God to forgive us. In the Bible, the word *"Repentance"* has several connotations:

1) To make an about face.
2)To change one's mind.
3) To feel sorrow.
Repentance involves our mind because we must make a decision to stop sinning. It involves our heart or our emotions because we feel sorrow for our sin, and it involves our will, because we make a decision to turn our back on sin.

In other words, it means you are sorry for that sin, and you have decided not to commit that sin anymore and to turn your back on it. FOR EXAMPLE: If you tell a lie, you would confess that sin to God and ask His forgiveness. It also means that you try your best not to lie anymore!

WHAT HAPPENS WHEN WE REPENT?

The Bible tells us that if we confess our sins to God, He is faithful and just to forgive and to cleanse us from **ALL** unrighteousness. When we repent, God forgives our sins! He takes sin out of our heart and cleans it up to get it ready for God's Spirit to move in.

OUR HEART IS LIKE A HOUSE. Look at your heart and imagine it as your house full of garbage with dirty dishes and trash scattered all over the place. You would not want your friends to see your house all messed up like that, would you? A filthy, dirty house is a picture of our heart when it is full of sin.

When we repent God cleans and washes our heart. He throws out the filth and sin that we find in ourselves. The good news is that God wants to live in your heart, but He wants to clean it up first!

As we found earlier, all of us have sinned. The wages of sin are death, and as a result of that sin, we should have had to die for our sin. But Jesus died because of our sin, In other words, He paid the price, or He died in our place. I do not have to die and be lost over my sins. Jesus took my place and made it possible for me to have everlasting life. On Calvary, He took my place!

HOW DO WE REPENT?

The Bible says that if we confess our sin, then God will forgive us. Confess means that we *"own up to"* or *"admit"* that a thing is true and to asseverate it to God. We must be willing to admit that we have sinned.

To repent, you might say something like this, "Dear Jesus, I love you with all my heart. I know that I have done wrong and I confess my sin to you. Please forgive and help me to never commit that sin again. In Jesus' Name I pray, Amen"

When you have repented and Jesus has forgiven your sin, you should feel a wonderful spirit of joy and thanks giving. All guilt and condemnation are gone! It is wonderful to know that your sins are forgiven you and that God has promised never to remember them against you anymore.

NOW THAT I HAVE REPENTED, WHAT HAPPENS NEXT?

After you have repented, there are two very important things that should take place in your life. Do you remember that your heart is like a house? When Jesus forgives you of your sins, your heart is now clean. However, it is also empty. But that is good because it means that sin is gone and that you are ready to be baptized in Jesus' name and to be filled with the Holy Ghost!

Some people are baptized after they receive the Holy Ghost, and others baptized first. But after God has forgiven your sins, you are ready to be baptized and to be filled with the Holy Ghost!

SIN AND CONFESSION OF SIN Romans 3:23

Romans 5:12
Romans 6:23
1 John 1:9
Proverbs 28:13
Galatians 5: 19-21
2 Corinthians 5:10
Hebrews 9:27

THE HEART IS LIKE A HOUSE Matthew 12: 43-44

Ephesians 2: 20-22
1 Corinthians 3: 16-17

REPENTANCE AND FORGIVENESS Mark 1: 3-4

Mark 1: 14-15
Mark 6:12
Luke 24:47
Acts 2:38
Acts 3: 19
Acts 20: 20-21
2 Peter 3:9
1 John 1:9
Isaiah 43:25
Micah 7:19

PEOPLE IN THE BIBLE WHO PREACHED REPENTANCE John the Baptist – Matthew 3:1-2

Jesus – Matthew 4:17
The Apostles – Mark 14:15
The Disciples of Jesus
Mark 6:10-12
Luke 13:3

WATER BAPTISM IN THE NAME OF JESUS

In the New Testament we find that baptism was a very important part of the early church. In this summary, we will see in Word and practice how the Apostles baptized believers. We will see that they baptized converts in the

Name of Jesus Christ, by submersion into water.

WHAT DOES THE WORD BAPTIZE MEAN?

The Word *"baptize"* means *"to dip"* or *"immerse"*, and that this is one reason we believe that believers should be put under water when they are baptized. That is what the word means. We also know that we should be baptized in water because that is how Jesus and His followers did it in the Bible.

HOW DO WE KNOW WE SHOULD BE BAPTIZED?

Jesus is the first one to tell us we needed to be baptized in His name. He also told His apostles that they should baptize their converts in Jesus' name.

Matthew 28:19, *"Go ye therefore…baptizing…"*
Mark 16:16, *"He that believeth and is baptized shall be saved…"*

JESUS WAS BAPTIZED

According to the Bible, John the Baptist baptized his converts in water. He even baptized Jesus. We know that Jesus was put under water because Matthew says that after He was baptized He *"went straight way out of the water" and saw the spirit of God descending like a dove.* Jesus was not baptized because He had sinned. He was baptized to set an example for us. (John 1:29-33, Matthew 3:13-17).

THEY WERE BAPTIZED ON THE DAY OF PENTECOST

When the church first came into the world, it happened on the day of Pentecost. We know that on that day they were baptized in the Name of Jesus Christ. The followers of Jesus had been instructed by Him to go to the city of Jerusalem and wait for the promise of the Father.

Acts chapter one tells us who was there when the Holy Ghost fell in the upper room. There were about 120 people there including the Apostles and Mary the mother of Jesus. The second chapter of Acts tells us what happened. We know that the Spirit of God fell on them and they were all filled with the Holy Ghost.

When the people gathered around they say and heard what had happened, they wanted to know how they could receive the same thing. That is when the Apostle Peter said, *"…repent and be baptized every one of you in the Name of Jesus Christ, for the remission of sins…"* And that they would also receive the Holy Ghost. (Acts chapter one and two)

CORNELIUS AND HIS HOUSEHOLD WERE BAPTIZED

In Acts chapter ten we read how God sent the Apostle peter to the house of Cornelius to preach the Gospel to them. Cornelius was a Gentile and they had not yet received the Gospel. He was a good man that really loved God, but he was not yet saved. (Acts 11:14)

While the Apostle Peter was preaching to them, Cornelius was filled with the Holy Ghost and then was baptized in the Name of Jesus. This shows us that even people who love god and do good things for Him need to be baptized. (Acts 10:45-48).

BELIEVERS AT EPHESUS ARE BAPTIZED

In Acts chapter nineteen we find some men there who already believe in Jesus. John the Baptist had already baptized them, but not in Jesus' name. When the Apostle Paul prayed for them they received the Holy Ghost and were baptized again in the Name of Jesus.

So we see that people who believed in Jesus must be baptized in the name of Jesus Christ. Even people, who have been baptized the wrong way, must be re-baptized in the Name of Jesus.

WHAT HAPPENS WHEN WE ARE BAPTIZED?

The Bible tells us we are baptized in the Name of Jesus Christ for the remission of our sins. The word *"remission'* means, *"to pardon"* or to let a guilty person go free. When you repent, Jesus forgives you and your sins. When you are baptized, your sins are remitted. This means that you are free from that sin and will not have to be punished (Acts 2:38; Luke 24:47).

WATER BAPTISM IS PART OF THE NEW BIRTH

Jesus told Nicodemus that we must be *"BORN AGAIN"* in order to enter into the Kingdom of God. We know that we cannot be saved unless we are in God's Kingdom. Therefore, we need to know what it means to be born again. Jesus said that we must be born again of, *"Water and Spirit"*; in John 3:5 he made it lucid. He was talking about a Spiritual birth that put us in the Kingdom of God. This means that we must be baptized in water in the Name of Jesus.

HOW SHOULD WE BE BAPTIZED?

We already know that we should be baptized by being immersed under water. But what should the preacher say over us when we are baptized? In every case in the Bible where it actually tells us what was said, we find that they were baptized in the Name of Jesus.

THE GIFT OF THE HOLY GHOST

"Then Peter said unto them, repent, and be baptized every one of you in the name of Jesus Christ for the remission of sins, and ye shall receive the GIFT OF THE GHOST."
Acts 2:38

GOD HAS A GIFT FOR YOU

Everyone likes to receive gifts. That is part of what we enjoy about birthdays and Christmas. A gift is something someone gives to you. You do not have to buy nor beg for a gift. It is freely given. (Matthew 10:8; Acts 10:45; Romans 3:24; 8:32; 1 Corinthians 2:12; 2 Corinthians 11:7).

WHAT IS THIS GIFT

What is the gift of the Holy Ghost? The Holy Ghost is the Spirit of God! We can see that the Holy Ghost is not an "It" but God Himself! God is a Spirit. He wants to be "in us" and not just "with" us. The gift of the Holy Ghost is God living in our hearts! (John 14:17; 1 Corinthians 3:16; Ephesians 4:8; Colossians 1:27; 1 Thessalonians 4:8).
Why is He called the Holy Ghost? The Bible tells us that God is Holy! He is perfect and pure in every sense. The word "Ghost" is just another way of saying "Spirit." So you can say Holy Ghost or Holy Spirit (1 Peter 1:16).

Do we need to be filled with the Holy Ghost to be saved? Yes! The reason is that the Holy Ghost is the Spirit of God. We must have His spirit to be saved. We need god's Spirit to live free from the flesh and sin. We also need the Holy Ghost in us to be resurrected (Romans 8:5-11; 1 Corinthians 15:35-58).

HOW TO RECEIVE THE GIFT OF THE HOLY GHOST

The Holy Ghost is a gift that must be accepted. Jesus will not violate your free will by forcing His Spirit on you. You must want God's Spirit in your heart.

1. **YOU MUST BELIEVE:** Jesus said, *"He that believeth on me as the scripture hath said, out of his belly shall flow rivers of living waters. (But this spake he of the Spirit, that they that believe on him should receive.)"*

2. **YOU MUST HAVE FAITH:** Hebrews 11:6 tells us that *"…without faith it is impossible to please him."* God rewards faith.

3. **YOU MUST ASK:** You can ask for the Holy Ghost to let God know that you want it, but you should not beg for it. (Matthew 7:7; Matthew 21:22) Jesus said in Luke 11:13, "*…how much more shall your heavenly Father give the Holy Ghost to them that ask him?*"

4. **YOU MUST REPENT:** We are commanded by John the Baptist, Jesus and the Apostles to repent, (Matthew 3: 1-2; Matthew 4:17; Luke 13:3; Acts 2:38).

5. **YOU MUST WORSHIP GOD:** It is important to worship God with your voice. God will not do for you what you can do for yourself. You must also worship God sincerely from the heart. When you worship God, you should use words of praise. As we worship God with our heart, the Spirit of God will take over and speak through you, "*…in other tongues, as the Spirit gives utterances*" (Acts 2:4).

HOW DO I KNOW I HAVE RECEIVED THE HOLY GHOST?

That is a good question. The gift of the Holy Ghost is so important that God wanted you to KNOW, without any doubt, when you receive it. Therefore, God speaks through you in another tongue that you do not know.

When we read the Bible what actually happened when someone received the Holy Ghost, we know that they spoke in tongues. Speaking in tongue as God gives the utterances is a supernatural sign to you that you have been filled with the Holy Ghost (Acts 2:4; Acts 10: 44-46; Acts 19:16).

WHAT WE MEAN WHEN WE SAY

Here are a few terms and expressions that are often heard in our services. We try to use these terms and expressions as the Bible uses them. Our hope is that this information will be helpful as you worship God.

AMEN: A Hebrew exclamation meaning "so be it," "truly," or "indeed!" It is often used to conclude prayer or to express approval or agreement with what someone has said or done, (see Deuteronomy 27:15; Revelations 22:20; 1 Corinthians 14: 16-17).

BAPTISM: Literally, the act of dipping or washing something completely in liquid. Scripture baptism is a vital part of New Testament salvation, (see Romans 6: 3-4; Galatians 3:27; 1Peter 3:21). It includes:

1. Water (Acts 8:36)
2. Much Water (john 3:23)
3. Going down into the water (Acts 8:38)
4. Burial in water (Colossians 2:12)
5. Coming up out of the water (Acts 8:39)
6. A name pronounced (Matthew 28:19; Acts 2:38)

Taking all of this information together, Scriptural baptism is total immersion in water in the name of Jesus Christ. Matthew 28:19 commands us to baptize in the name but does not give the name. It refers to the ""name of the Father, and of the Son and of the Holy Ghost." The terms Father, Son and Holy Ghost are titles of positions held by God, but they are not proper names. Jesus is the only name that is connected with salvation (Matthew 1:21; Acts 4:12). Acts 2:38 records the apostles' fulfillment of the command of Matthew 28:19 and gives the Scriptural formula for baptism in the New Testament Church: *"Repent and be baptized in the name of Jesus Christ for the remission of sins."*

BAPTISM OF THE HOLY GHOST: Literally, being dipped, plunged or immersed in the Spirit of God. The baptism of the Holy Ghost is the birth of the Spirit and thus is a vital part of entrance into the kingdom of God, (see John 3:5). The initial evidence of the baptism of the Spirit is speaking in other tongues (languages) as the Spirit of God gives utterance, (see Acts 2:4).

Joel and Isaiah both prophesied this experience (Isaiah 28; 11-12; Joel 2: 28-29). It was foretold by John the Baptist (Matthew 3:11), purchased by the blood of Jesus and promised by Him to His followers (John 14:26; 15:26). The Holy Ghost was first poured out on the Day of Pentecost on the Jews (Acts 2: 1- 41). Later Samaritans received this experience (Acts 8:17) and the Gentiles (Acts 10:44-46; 19:6).

BORN AGAIN: To start over, to begin life with a fresh start. Jesus used this expression to describe what takes place through faith in Him when a person is baptized in water in His name and receives the Holy Ghost (birth of water and of spirit), see (John 3: 1-8; Acts 2:38). According to Jesus, without this fresh start no one can enter into the Kingdom of God.

CHRIST: a Greek word meaning "the anointed One," equivalent to the Hebrew word Messiah. New Testament believers use it exclusively to refer to Jesus Christ of Nazareth, who fulfilled the Old Testament prophecies concerning the Messiah and became our Savior.

CHRISTIAN: A description of believers in Jesus Christ that means "like Christ" or "belonging to Christ." It describes the object of our faith and loyalty, the One with whom we want to be identified. It is not intended to be an exclusive or sectarian term, (see Acts 11:26; 1Peter 4: 12-16).

DELIVERANCE: Being set free from something that has one bound. Jesus promised deliverance as a part of His Messianic work (Luke 4:18).

DISCIPLE: A follower or a student; in our case, we have voluntarily chosen to become a follower of Jesus and adhere to His teaching. A disciple learns from his teachers and endeavors to spread the teacher's message to others, (Matthew 28: 18-20; Luke 14:27; John 15: 1-8).

DIVINE HEALING: The divine intervention of God to cure sickness of body and mind. Divine healing was purchased for us by the blood of Jesus that flowed from His stripes (Isaiah 53:5; Matthew 8; 16-17; 1Peter 2:24). Jesus went everywhere healing those who were sick (Matthew 4:23-24), and He commanded His apostles to do the same. He said to those who believe the gospel, *"They shall lay hands on the sick, and they shall recover"* (Mark 16:18). Mighty healings and miracles followed the disciples wherever the gospel was preached. Healing is available to us today (James 5: 14-16).

FELLOWSHIP: Based on a Biblical term meaning to share or have in common; similar to our concept of close friendship. Fellowship is linked in Scripture with love, compassion, a willingness to bear one another's in Scripture with love, compassion, a willingness to bear one another's 47; Philippians 2: 1-11).

GODHEAD: The divine essence; deity; the fullness of God's character and attributes. The Bible teaches that there is only one God (Deuteronomy 6:4). He is a Spirit (John 4:24), and He has manifested Himself in flesh as Jesus Christ (1 Timothy 3:16). He now baptizes us with His Spirit so that we can be the children of God.

HALLELUJAH: AHebrew word meaning "praise the Lord" or "Praise Yahweh, Jehovah" (Psalms 150: 1, 6).

HOLINESS: Separation from sin and dedication to God. When we come to the Lord we are to forsake sin (John 8:11). We are to *"Live righteously, and godly, in this present world,"* (Titus 2:12). Without holiness no one shall see the Lord (Hebrews 12:14). We must present ourselves as holy unto God, (Romans 12:1), cleanse ourselves from all filthiness of flesh and spirit (2 Corinthians 7:1), separate ourselves from all worldliness (James 4:4). The

Scripture is clear that no one can live a holy life by his own power, but only through the Holy Spirit (Acts 1:8; Romans 8:4).

YAHWEH: The personal name of Almighty God in the Old Testament. The exact meaning is debated, but is relatedto the Hebrew phrase "I AM." As such, it reveals God's self-existence and lack of dependence on anything or anyone else (Exodus 3: 13-15; Deuteronomy 6: 4-5; John 8: 54-59).

JESUS: It is a name that literally means "Yahweh Savior," Yahweh saves," or "Yahweh has become our salvation." In the New Testament it is the supreme name b y which God revealed Himself when He came in flesh. It is *"the only name under heaven given among men whereby we must be saved"* (Acts 4:12). Paul commanded, *"Whatsoever you do in word or deed, do all in the name of the Lord Jesus"* (Colossians 3:17).

LORD'S SUPPER: The practice of eating bread and drinking the fruit of the vine together as an act of worship and remembrance. Jesus began this practice at His last supper with His disciples. It is a time to remember what Jesus has done for us, to examine our own lives and faith and to recommit ourselves to Jesus in greater faithfulness. It is also called communion (from the term meaning to share together). It is to be observed as often as each individual church deems appropriate, but it must not be ignored (Matthew 26: 17-30; 1 Corinthians 11: 17-34).

OFFERING: It is the voluntary collection of monetary gifts to support the work of the church and various ministries-locally, nationally and internationally. Properly viewed, the offering is an expression of love and gratitude for the blessings of God (1 Corinthians 16: 1-2; 2 Corinthians 9: 6-9).

PASTOR: Literally, one who tends or shepherds a flock. The pastor is t he shepherd of the local part of God's flock (Ephesians 4:11).

PENTECOSTAL: An adjective used to describe those who have received the same experience that the followers of Jesus did on the Day of Pentecost (Acts 2: 1-4).

PRAISE: To speak or sing or make other expressions extolling, admiring or commending greatness and goodness of God. We typically lift our voices in praise to God, and sometimes we lift our hands in gesture of surrender to Him (Psalms 100:4; 147:1; Ephesians 5: 19-20; Hebrews 13:15; Colossians 3: 15-17).

PRAYER: Speaking to or communicating with God. We respond to God's invitation to bring our praise and gratitude as well as our concerns and needs. According to Jesus, prayer is like a child coming to a loving father. For prayer to be effective we must pray in faith and sincerity and not merely memorized words (Matthew 6: 5-15; James 5: 13-18).

RAPTURE: Literally, a "Catching away." In our context it refers to the time when the Lord will come back for His church. The church will be caught up to meet Him in the air (1 Thessalonians 4: 16-17).

REPENTANCE: A change of mind that brings about a change of behavior. It is the first step in the three-point plan that Peter gave when sinners asked at the close of his message on the Day of Pentecost, "What shall we do?" Repentance is a turn away from sin, a death to sin. By repentance we identify with the death of the Lord (Luke 13:3; Acts 2:38; 17:30; Romans 6: 1-2; 2 Peter 3:9).

GOSPEL: The death, burial and resurrection of the Lord, which receive by grace through faith (Ephesians 2: 8-9). The Gospel is the death, burial and resurrection of Jesus Christ (1 Corinthians 15: 1-4). When we truly believe the gospel, we will obey the gospel and apply it to our lives (Romans 16:26; 2 Thessalonians 1:8). We die with Him in repentance. We are buried with Him in Baptism. We are resurrected with Him to walk in newness of life by receiving the Spirit. Full salvation consists of repentance, baptism in Jesus' Name and baptism of the Holy Ghost (Acts 2:38; Romans 6: 1-7).

TITHES; A Biblical word meaning a tenth. We support God's ordained ministry and work and by giving a tenth of our income (Malachi 3:10; 1 Corinthians 16:2).

TONGUES: Speaking in tongue means speaking miraculously in a language unknown to the speaker. It occurs as the Spirit gives utterance (Acts 2:4), not by human learning or imitation. There are two major functions of speaking in tongues in the New Testament Church:

1. Speaking in tongues is the manifestation God has given as the definite, indisputable, supernatural witness or sign of the baptism of the Holy Ghost (Acts 2: 1-4; 10: 44-46; 19:6).

Isaiah prophesied that it would accompany the rest and refreshing) Isaiah 28: 11-12), and Jesus foretold it as a sign that would follow believers of the Gospel (Mark 16:17). Jews and Gentiles alike both received this experience.

2. Speaking in tongues is also a gift to believers after the initial baptism of the Holy Ghost (1 Corinthians 12: 1-10). Paul gave regulations for the use of tongues in public worship (1 Corinthians 14: 1-40). He explained that tongues is given both for self edification (1 Corinthians 14:4), and for the deification of the Church (1 Corinthians 14: 27-28).

In church meetings the gift of tongues is used to give a public message, which is meant to be interpreted (the gift of interpretation is another gift of the Spirit). Since the possibility for misuse exist, this gift needs proper regulation (1 Corinthians 14: 23-28). Not all believers have the gift of tongues for public use, which is different in function from the tongues that are the initial evidence of the Holy Ghost baptism (1 Corinthians 14: 18, 39).